T0196898

THE
FIVE HOLY HABITS

— Living as a Child of God —

The Brothers and Sisters of Jesus Christ
John 1:12

REV. DR. JON K. ANDERSON

WESTBOW
P R E S S®
A DIVISION OF THOMAS NELSON
& ZONDERVAN

WestBow Press books may be ordered through booksellers or by contacting:

WestBow Press
A Division of Thomas Nelson & Zondervan
1663 Liberty Drive
Bloomington, IN 47403
www.westbowpress.com
1 (866) 928-1240

ISBN: 978-1-5127-6855-8 (sc)
ISBN: 978-1-5127-6854-1 (e)

Library of Congress Control Number: 2016920754

Print information available on the last page.

WestBow Press rev. date: 07/26/2017

DEDICATION

This book is dedicated to my faithful Christian brother, Mark Dolde, and to the wonderful young men and women who lead the Koinonia Ministry at Concordia Lutheran High School in Fort Wayne, Indiana. Mark called me "Moses" and he was my "Aaron" as we developed the Koinonia Ministry. He and our young colleagues were an inspiration to us as we worked together to promote the Five Holy Habits at our school. May God richly bless you as you continue to work together as disciples of Jesus Christ.

FOREWORD

This book was originally written as a letter to my family and friends. The content is a product of my calling as a pastor and science teacher at Concordia Lutheran High School in Fort Wayne, Indiana. It is an outgrowth of the mandate I was given to develop a ministry at CLHS that would go beyond the classroom to help our young people put their faith into action.

The Five Holy Habits are the guiding principle that came out of developing the Koinonia Ministry. They are a distillation of our study of what it looks like to be a disciple of Jesus Christ. They are the core activities that shape the lives of God's children as they follow Jesus Christ, guided by the Holy Spirit.

The Five Holy Habits are Scripture, Prayer, Fellowship, Service, and Witness. They all involve interaction with others. Scripture and Prayer are the means by which we interact with God. God talks to us through the Bible and we talk to Him with our heart felt prayers. Fellowship, Koinonia in Greek, is Christians interacting with each other as they seek God's will for them - stirring each other up for love and good deeds. Service and Witness are how God's children interact with all people as they fulfill their calling to be Salt and Light in the world.

My prayer for you, as you read this book, is that it will clarify your mission in life as a Child of God. I pray that it will bless you in such a way that you will be an ever increasing blessing to others. God's grace and peace be with you.

INTRODUCTION

It's all about Jesus.

My dear family and friends -

I am writing this letter to you because I love you. I dearly want to spend eternity with you and I want you to have a rich full life now. As my years add up I feel an ever greater urging to share with you what I have come to believe and of which I am convinced. During my life I have become more and more certain that the only way for you to have what I deeply desire for you is for you to have an ever growing closer relationship with Jesus Christ - both as Savior and as Lord. Jesus truly is who He says He is - the Way, the Truth, and the Life. (John 14:6) I write this not because we haven't talked about faith in Jesus, not because I question your goodness or faith, but because I question my own inadequacy in sharing this ultimately important truth with you. No one can truly know the mind and heart of someone else..

Happiness, contentment, and joy in life comes from two things. 1. Knowing you are loved and 2. Knowing you are capable, willing, and actively giving love to others. A trusting, obedient relationship with Jesus Christ supplies both of these needs. Jesus said "I am the gate; whoever enters through me will be saved. He will come in and go out, and find pasture. The thief comes only to steal and kill and destroy; I have come that they may have life, and have it to the full. I am the good shepherd. The good shepherd lays down his life for the sheep." (John 10:9-11) Jesus is the perfect Son of God who came to earth to pay the price for our sin, to be sacrificed as the Lamb of God who takes away the sin of the world. "For God so loved the world that he gave his one and only Son, that whoever believes in him shall not perish but have eternal life." (John 3:16)

There is life after death, an eternal joyful existence in God's presence (heaven) or eternal tormenting absence from all God's goodness and blessings (hell). And trusting in Jesus is the only way to have eternal fellowship with God. Jesus truly is the ONLY way, truth, and life, the ONLY one through whom we have access to God the Father.

This faith that we have, called Christianity, is essentially a personal relationship with Jesus Christ. We trust in Jesus for our eternal welfare and for wisdom to guide us through life. Saint Paul wrote, "If you declare with your mouth, 'Jesus is Lord', and believe in your heart that God raised him from the dead, you will be saved" (Romans 10:9) "Jesus is Lord" is often called the earliest creed of the Christian church. This includes both an outward and an inward expression of our faith.

Before Jesus was born an angel spoke to Joseph about Mary. The angel said, "She will give birth to a son, and you are to give him the name Jesus, because he will save his people from their sin." (Matthew 1:21) Jesus, His name means "Savior." Jesus is also our Lord. A lord is a ruling authority. When we confess with the words "Jesus is Lord" we are actually saying "My Savior runs my life." We trust Jesus as Savior exclusively, without any merit of our own. We then follow Him as Lord, trusting Him to guide every aspect of our life.

You can always trust Jesus to be Lord of your life because He loves you more than you love yourself. We take our orders from Jesus and He said, "If you love me, keep my commands." (John 14:15) He also said, "Whoever has my commands and keeps them is the one who loves me. The one who loves me will be loved by my Father, and I too will love them and show myself to them." (John 14:21) But what is Christ's command for us? He said, "My command is this: Love each other as I have loved you." (John 15:12) Jesus even repeated it -- "This is my command: Love each other." (John 15:17) When Jesus was asked what was the greatest commandment in the law He replied, "Love the Lord your God with all your heart and with all your soul and with all your mind. This is the first and greatest commandment. And the second is like it: Love your neighbor as yourself. All the Law and the Prophets hang on these two commandments." (Matthew22:37-40) We show love for God by following His commands, by loving other people.

In order to love God by loving others we need to get our focus off of ourselves and onto God's will for us, but the world we live in is constantly trying to get us to focus on ourselves and what our sinful selves want. Jesus said to his disciples, "Whoever wants to be my disciple must deny themselves and take up their cross and follow me. For whoever wants to save their life will lose it, but whoever loses their life for me will find it. What good will it be for someone to gain the whole world, yet forfeit their soul? Or what can anyone give in exchange for their soul? For the Son of Man is going to come in his Father's glory with his angels, and then he will reward each person according to what they have done. (Matthew 16:24-27)

Chapter eleven of the book of Hebrews recounts the lives of faithful believers who trusted in God and trusted the message they heard from God. Then chapter twelve begins with, "Therefore, since we are surrounded by such a great cloud of witnesses, let us throw off everything that hinders and the sin that so easily entangles. And let us run with perseverance the race marked out for us, fixing our eyes on Jesus, the pioneer and perfecter of faith. For the joy set before him he endured the cross, scorning its shame, and sat down at the right hand of the throne of God. Consider him who endured such opposition from sinners, so that you will not grow weary and lose heart." (Hebrews 12:1-3) There is also "joy set before you" as a faithful follower of Jesus Christ.

As a disciple of Jesus we have Him as our teacher who teaches us with His life as well as with His words. On the very night in which He was betrayed He taught His disciples with words and actions as He took the place of a servant and washed their feet. After He had finished he said to them, "Now that I, your Lord and Teacher, have washed your feet, you also should wash one another's feet. I have set you an example that you should do as I have done for you. Very truly I tell you, no servant is greater than his master, nor is a messenger greater than the one who sent him. Now that you know these things, you will be blessed if you do them." (John 13:14-17)

The Apostle Paul had his eyes fixed on Jesus and followed

Christ's example. (1Corinthians 11:1) As Christians we have a perfect example and model for living a God pleasing and blessed life. "Follow God's example, therefore, as dearly loved children and walk in the way of love, just as Christ loved us and gave himself up for us as a fragrant offering and sacrifice to God." (Ephesians 5:1) I pray that you will always live with your eyes fixed on Jesus.

Saint Paul wrote to his fellow Christians to remind them of what they had been taught. He wrote, "Now, brothers and sisters, I want to remind you of the gospel I preached to you, which you received and on which you have taken your stand." (1Corinthians 15:1) Saint Peter did the same. He wrote, "So I will always remind you of these things, even though you know them and are firmly established in the truth you now have." (2Peter 1:12) "Dear friends, this is now my second letter to you. I have written both of them as reminders to stimulate you to wholesome thinking. (2Peter 3:1) Peter's last recorded words are, "Therefore, dear friends, since you have been forewarned, be on your guard so that you may not be carried away by the error of the lawless and fall from your secure position. But grow in the grace and knowledge of our Lord and Savior Jesus Christ. To him be glory both now and forever! Amen." (2Peter 3:17-18) With this letter, I am seeking to remind you of these same things, my dearly loved family and friends.

With this in mind there are some more specific activities in living the Christian life for which I would like to remind you. We have three great enemies that are constantly trying to get us to forget the truths that Jesus taught us - the devil, the world, and our own sinful desires. So we need to be constantly reminded of who Jesus is and what He taught.

And we have such a person to do that for us - the Holy Spirit. Jesus promised the Spirit's presence in our lives with these words, "But the Advocate, the Holy Spirit, whom the Father will send in my name, will teach you all things and will remind you of everything I have said to you." (John 14:26) As God's children we have the Spirit to help us whenever we ask. Jesus taught, "Which of you fathers, if your son asks for a fish, will give him a snake instead?Or if he asks for an egg, will give him a scorpion? If you then, though you are evil, know how to give good gifts to your children, how much more will your Father in heaven give the Holy Spirit to those who ask him!" (Like 11:11-13) As a child of God, He promises you the gift of the Holy Spirit for the asking. So ask!

Jesus warned about our three great enemies in the parable of the Sower, Matthew 13:1-23. The devil, with his lies, tries to snatch away the seeds of God's truth before it can take root in our hearts. The world tries to get shallow Christians to deny Christ with its heat of ridicule, persecution, and ostracism. Our own sinful desires try to crowd out our devotion to Christ with worries and pleasures. But Jesus tells us, "So do not worry, saying, 'What shall we eat?' or 'What shall we drink?' or 'What shall we wear?' For the pagans run after all these things, and your heavenly Father knows that you need them. But seek first his kingdom and his righteousness, and all these things will be given to you as well. Therefore do not worry about tomorrow, for tomorrow will worry about itself. Each day has enough trouble of its own." (Matthew 6:31-34) Jesus has yesterday, today, and forever firmly in His grasp. Trust Him!

All personal relationships result from interactions

between people. We interact through conversations and through activities done together. We are also able to have a personal relationship with Jesus Christ by talking with Him and through putting what He teaches us into practice in our lives. Our conversations with Jesus are done through the Holy Bible and through prayer. Jesus talks to us through the Scriptures and we talk to Him through our prayers. Indeed, Jesus is called "God's Word" by the Apostle John. -- "In the beginning was the Word, [Jesus] and the Word was with God, and the Word was God." (John 1:1) Through Christian Scriptures and through prayer to the triune God of Scripture we grow in our relationship to the one true God. When we interact with other Christians with Scripture and prayer we grow in our relationship to each other and we "spur one another on toward love and good deeds." (Hebrews 10:24) We then become the Salt and Light that is a blessing to the world and moves the world toward faith in Jesus Christ.

These are the five Holy Habits in the life of a Christian. They involve both interaction with God and interaction with other Christians which strengthen our faith in Jesus Christ and produce the actions characteristic of a child of God. We have interaction with God through Scripture and Prayer. We have interaction with other Christians through the fellowship of worship and interactive Bible study. When we interact with God and His family it stirs us up for loving actions and joyful living. We share our joy with others through Service and Witnessing.

[5 Holy Habits = Interact (S,P,F) + Act (S,W)]
My dear family and friends, TRUST JESUS.

SCRIPTURE

God talks to us.

"Above all, you must understand that no prophecy of Scripture came about by the prophet's own interpretation of things. For prophecy never had its origin in the human will, but prophets, though human, spoke from God as they were carried along by the Holy Spirit." (2Peter 1:20-21) These words from the apostle Peter assure us that the Bible is the very words of God which He has given us to know the truth about Him and to guide us through the life that He has given us. The Bible helps us to understand our place in the whole human race, it helps us to know why we exist, it assures us of God's love, and it gives us direction for interacting with God, other people, and His whole creation.

I began my serious study of God's Word when I was about twelve years old. Any of the good that I have done in this life I attribute to the Holy Spirit working in me through God's word. Anything that I have done wrong is a result of my ignoring or forgetting to follow God's Word. God's Word truly has been "A lamp unto my feet, and a light unto my path." (Psalm 119:105) These are the two lights that emanate from God's Word. We call these Lights the Law and the Gospel. When we are without God's Word it is like being lost in the woods during a dark night. The Light of the Law is like a flashlight that we hold in our hands. It keeps us from stumbling over the rocks and exposed roots in life that rob us of a joyful fruitful life. The flashlight of the Law, however, only keeps us from stumbling in this life, it does not lead us to heaven. The Path to heaven requires a Light that is beyond us. It is like a campfire that we can see at a distance that leads out of the dark woods to our Home. This campfire Light is the Gospel of Jesus Christ - the only way home.

All Scripture, when it is taken as a whole, leads us into a closer relationship with Jesus Christ. Jesus told the Jewish leaders, "You study the Scriptures diligently because you think that in them you possess eternal life. These are the very Scriptures that testify about me, yet you refuse to come to me to have life." (John 5:39-40) The heart of the Christian faith is a relationship with Jesus Christ resulting in the confession "Jesus is Lord." (Romans 10:9) The name Jesus means "Savior" and Lord places Him as a ruler, a "King". The ruler of a kingdom that is not of this world. (John 18:36) When your relationship to Jesus Christ is formulated in the confession "Jesus is Lord", in effect you are saying, "My Savior runs my life." Jesus spoke of this relationship when He said, "Anyone who loves me will obey my teaching. My Father will love them, and we will come to them and make our home with them. Anyone who does not love me will not obey my teaching. These words you hear are not my own; they belong to the Father who sent me." (John 14:23-24)

We learn and can then obey Christ's teaching by reading

the Bible and then putting it into practice in our lives. This is not to say that our own efforts alone are able to accomplish this. Indeed we need supernatural help to believe, to confess, and to obey Jesus. As He said, "All this I have spoken while still with you. But the Advocate, the Holy Spirit, whom the Father will send in my name, will teach you all things and will remind you of everything I have said to you." (John 14:25-26) Indeed, God's Word is the "sword of the Spirit" that enables us to battle the devil, worldliness, and our own sinful desires. (Ephesians 6:17) Indeed, Jesus Himself kept quoting God's word from the Holy Scriptures as He battled the devil when tempted in the wilderness.

Saint Paul emphasized this relationship between faith in Jesus and the Bible when he wrote to Timothy these words: "But as for you, continue in what you have learned and have become convinced of, because you know those from whom you learned it, and how from infancy you have known the Holy Scriptures, which are able to make you wise for salvation through faith in Christ Jesus. All Scripture is God-breathed and is useful for teaching, rebuking, correcting and training in righteousness, so that the servant of God may be thoroughly equipped for every good work." (2Timothy 3:14-17) The Bible contains all that we need to know in order to live the life of a child of God.

There are two great pitfalls that bring disaster into the life of the Christian. They are polar opposites; they are pride and despair. The Law and the Gospel, as given to us in the Holy Scriptures, serve to keep us from falling into either of these pits. The Law of God destroys our pride as it sets the pattern of a righteous life. When we compare our own life to the pattern given to us by God in the Law, it destroys our pride. When we read of God's love for us in the Gospel, the sacrificial death of God's only begotten Son, it eliminates the despair that destroys our hope. It leads us away from a hopeless end toward an endless hope. As the Bible tells us concerning this hope, it "does not put us to shame, because God's love has been poured out into our hearts through the Holy Spirit, who has been given to us." (Romans 5:5) The Bible is like the best kind of friend who lovingly points out faults and also encourages us to be all that God has called us to be.

The last word of Saint Peter, given to us by the Holy Spirit in the Bible, are an exhortation to continual growth in our faith. He wrote in 2Peter 3:18, "But grow in grace, and in the knowledge of our Lord and Savior Jesus Christ. To him be glory both now and for ever. Amen." We grow in knowledge by reading and believing the Holy Scriptures. We grow in grace by trusting in His promises and applying God's Word to our lives. As we read, believe, and act in faith we become more secure in our place in God's family and we walk with Jesus as one of His disciples. As Jesus told the Jews who believed in Him, "If you hold to my teaching, you are really my disciples. Then you will know the truth, and the truth will set you free." (John 8:31-32) God wants His children to know the truth about ourselves and about the relationship that He desires to have with us.

Listening to God through His Word is the foundation for living the blessed Christian life. It is the foundation upon which we build our life of faith. It provides guidance for the other four Holy Habits. It prepares us to live as one of God's beloved children. It enables us to be a blessing to others. It prepares us for the many challenges that we will

4

face in life. Jesus made this clear at the end of His Sermon on the Mount - "Therefore everyone who hears these words of mine and puts them into practice is like a wise man who built his house [his life] on the rock. The rain came down, the streams rose, and the winds blew and beat against that house; yet it did not fall, because it had its foundation on the rock." (Matthew 7:24-25) I pray that you will have a rock solid faith in Jesus Christ as Savior and Lord.

My dear family and friends, LIVE ACCORDING TO GOD'S WORD.

PRAYER

We talk to God

One of the most beautiful things about our Christian faith is that we know God as a being who wants to interact with us, to be ever present in our lives. God became human in the form of Jesus Christ. As the Apostle John tells us, "The Word became flesh and made his dwelling among us. We have seen his glory, the glory of the one and only Son, who came from the Father, full of grace and truth." (John 1:14) Unlike every other religion Christianity is not a set of rules or laws that must be obeyed in order to be acceptable to God. The Christian faith draws us into a relationship with God. John also tells us that through faith in Jesus we become God's children. He wrote, "Yet to all who did receive him, to those who believed in his name, he gave the right to become children of God - children born not of natural descent, nor of human decision or a husband's will, but born of God." (John 1:12-13)

Jesus taught us that His Father is our Father. Jesus is a Christian's teacher, brother, and friend. Jesus is also our great prophet, priest, and king. Believers have a personal relationship with God, the Triune God - Father, Son, and

Holy Spirit. And just as every human relationship involves interaction, as God's children we are invited into personal interaction with our God. That is really what prayer is all about. In prayer we approach the very throne of God, our God who loved us so much that He became flesh in order to be sacrificed for our salvation. As the author of Hebrews puts it, "For we do not have a high priest who is unable to empathize with our weaknesses, but we have one who has been tempted in every way, just as we are - yet he did not sin. Let us then approach God's throne of grace with confidence, so that we may receive mercy and find grace to help us in our time of need." (Hebrews 4:15-16) Jesus is our perfect advocate with our Father in heaven. Because He became one of us, He has an intimate relationship with our human condition and knows our needs better than we know them ourselves.

Through the reading of Scripture and through prayer we carry on an ongoing conversation with God. He addresses us through His Word and we address Him through our prayers. Jesus taught that those who believe in Him are God's children and that we can address God as our loving Father. When the disciples asked Jesus to teach them how to pray, He taught them to pray to "Our Father who art in heaven." The *our* indicates a family relationship between believers and God. Jesus said, "This, then, is how you should pray: 'Our Father in heaven, hallowed be your name, your kingdom come, your will be done, on earth as it is in heaven. Give us today our daily bread. And forgive us our debts, as we also have forgiven our debtors. And lead us not into temptation, but deliver us from the evil one." (Matthew

6:9-13) This prayer that Jesus taught us perfectly expresses our needs as they are addressed to our loving Father in heaven.

Christian believers throughout all the ages have demonstrated for us the importance of prayer in their lives. "Isaac prayed to the LORD on behalf of his wife, because she was childless. The LORD answered his prayer, and his wife Rebekah became pregnant." (Genesis 25:21) David was a man of prayer. As recorded in Scripture - "Then King David went in and sat before the LORD, and he said: 'Who am I, Sovereign LORD, and what is my family, that you have brought me this far?'" (2Samuel 7:18) Hezekiah prayed for healing from an illness that could have led to his death. God told the prophet Isaiah, "Go back and tell Hezekiah, the ruler of my people, 'This is what the LORD, the God of your father David, says: I have heard your prayer and seen your tears; I will heal you. On the third day from now you will go up to the temple of the LORD.'" (2Kings 20:5) Jesus modeled a life of prayer. We read in Hebrews, "During the days of Jesus' life on earth, he offered up prayers and petitions with fervent cries and tears to the one who could save him from death, and he was heard because of his reverent submission." (Hebrews 5:7) God always hears the prayers of His children and answers them. He gives us exactly what we need for every situation in life.

We are also told by Saint Luke that the early believers "all joined together constantly in prayer, along with the women and Mary the mother of Jesus, and his brothers." (Acts 1:14) A Christian's prayer not only comes into God's presence with requests but also with adoration, confession, and thanksgiving. It calms our fears knowing that our Father in heaven hears us and will do whatever is best for us. Paul told the Christians at Philippi, "Do not be anxious about anything, but in every situation, by prayer and petition, with thanksgiving, present your requests to God. And the peace of God, which transcends all understanding, will guard your hearts and your minds in Christ Jesus." (Philippians 4:6-7) Prayer to our Father brings peace because we know that He is listening and will respond in a way that perfectly fits our circumstances.

Jesus said, referring to prayer, "Ask and it will be given to you; seek and you will find; knock and the door will be opened to you. For everyone who asks receives; the one who seeks finds; and to the one who knocks, the door will be opened." (Matthew 7:7-8) Jesus also said, "If you remain in me and my words remain in you, ask whatever you wish, and it will be done for you. This is to my Father's glory, that you bear much fruit, showing yourselves to be my disciples." (John 15:7-8) These words indicate that prayer is also the Christians preparation for taking action, for doing those things that fulfill our calling to be the Salt of the earth and the Light of the world.

The greatest gift from God that Christians need to ask for is the gift of the Holy Spirit. Before Jesus left us in the body, not in spirit, He promised to send us the Holy Spirit . He said, "But the Advocate, the Holy Spirit, whom the Father will send in my name, will teach you all things and will remind you of everything I have said to you." (John 14:26) Jesus also taught us that it is God's great desire to send us His Spirit. He said, "Which of you fathers, if your son asks for a fish, will give him a snake instead? Or if he asks for an egg, will give him a scorpion? If you then, though you are evil, know how to give good gifts to your children, how much more will your Father in heaven give the Holy Spirit to those who ask him!" (Like 11:11-13) Just as we need good food to live a healthy physical life, we need God's Spirit in order to live a healthy spiritual life.

The Holy Spirit helps us to communicate with our Father in prayer. As Paul taught, "The Spirit helps us in our weakness. We do not know what we ought to pray for, but the Spirit himself intercedes for us through wordless groans." (Romans 8:26) And he told the Ephesians, "And pray in the Spirit on all occasions with all kinds of prayers and requests. With this in mind, be alert and always keep on praying for all the Lord's people." (Ephesians 6:18) God's Spirit dwells in every child of God and is our constant helper in prayer, comforting us with the assurance that God hears our prayers, He knows our need, and that He will supply exactly what is required to help us in every situation.

Paul prayed for those who came to faith in Christ through his preaching of the Gospel. He told them, "This is my prayer: that your love may abound more and more in knowledge and depth of insight, so that you may be able to discern what is best and may be pure and blameless for the day of Christ, filled with the fruit of righteousness that comes through Jesus Christ to the glory and praise of God." (Philippians 1:9-11) We, too, need to pray for each other. This enriches our fellowship and prepares us to work together to accomplish the work that He gives us to do.

On the night in which He was betrayed, at the Passover feast, Jesus prayed for Himself, and for the disciples. He also prayed for you and me and all who come to faith in Him. He said, "My prayer is not for them alone. I pray also for those who will believe in me through their message, that all of them may be one, Father, just as you are in me and I am in you. May they also be in us so that the world may believe that you have sent me." (John 17:20-21) Prayer is the bond that keeps us in intimate fellowship with God and with our brothers and sisters in Christ.

My dear family and friends, BE ALWAYS PRAYING.

FELLOWSHIP

Our family meetings

Christian fellowship, Scriptural and prayerful interactions between Christians, is an essential ingredient for Christian growth and effectiveness in Christian living. It is a oneness in mind and spirit that brings unity for putting our faith into action. Jesus prayed for this kind of unity for us when he said, "My prayer is not for them alone. I pray also for those who will believe in me through their message, that all of them may be one, Father, just as you are in me and I am in you. May they also be in us so that the world may believe that you have sent me." (John 17:20-21)

The first Christians met together continually for strength, encouragement, and caring. Luke writes, "They [the first Christians] devoted themselves to the apostles' teaching and to fellowship, to the breaking of bread and to prayer. Everyone was filled with awe at the many wonders and signs performed by the apostles. All the believers were together and had everything in common. They sold property and possessions to give to anyone who had need. Every day they continued to meet together in the temple courts. They broke bread in their homes and ate together with glad and sincere hearts, praising God and enjoying the favor of all the people. And the Lord added to their number daily those who were being saved." (Acts 2:42-47) This same kind of Christian fellowship is essential for effective ministry today. These first Christians are a model that we are given so that we can carry on the mission that they started.

It is through Christian fellowship that we develop relationships with each other and with each of the persons of the Holy Trinity. It is a relationship based on a loving obedience to Jesus Christ. As Jesus said, "If you love me, keep my commands. And I will ask the Father, and he will give you another advocate to help you and be with you forever - the Spirit of truth. The world cannot accept him, because it neither sees him nor knows him. But you know him, for he lives with you and will be in you. I will not leave you as orphans; I will come to you. Before long, the world will not see me anymore, but you will see me. Because I live, you also will live. On that day you will realize that I am in my Father, and you are in me, and I am in you. Whoever has my commands and keeps them is the one who loves me. The one who loves me will be loved by my Father, and I too will love them and show myself to them." (John 14:15-21) This fellowship is not simply an association of like-minded people, it is a fellowship of God's family with each other and with the powerful and inspiring presence of God Himself.

The Bible uses two significant and instructive analogies to help us to understand what true Christian fellowship is. It compares Christians relationships to each other as parts of a body. It also describes each Christian's physical body as a temple as well as depicting our relationship to each other in the body of Christ as a larger temple. Paul extensively employs the analogy of Christian fellowship to a body in first Corinthians.

> Just as a body, though one, has many parts, but all its many parts form one body, so it is with Christ. For we were all baptized by one Spirit so as to form one body whether Jews or Gentiles, slave or free, and we were all given the one Spirit to drink. Even so the body is not made up of one part but of many. Now if the foot should say, "Because I am not a hand, I do not belong to the body," it would not for that reason stop being part of the body. And if the ear should say, "Because I am not an eye, I do not belong to the body," it would not for that reason stop being part of the body. If the whole body were an eye, where would the sense of hearing be? If the whole body were an ear, where would the sense of smell be? But in fact God has placed the parts in the body, every one of them, just as he wanted them to be. If they were all one part, where would the body be? As it is, there are many parts, but one body. The eye cannot say to the hand, "I don't need you! And the head cannot say to the feet, "I don't need you!" On the contrary, those parts of the body that seem to be weaker are indispensable, and the parts that we think are less honorable we treat with special

honor. And the parts that are unpresentable are treated with special modesty, while our presentable parts need no special treatment. But God has put the body together, giving greater honor to the parts that lacked it, so that there should be no division in the body, but that its parts should have equal concern for each other. If one part suffers, every part suffers with it; if one part is honored, every part rejoices with it. Now you are the body of Christ, and each one of you is a part of it. (1Corinthians 12:12-27)

This analogy helps us to realize that as Christians we need each other and we need to be able to work together. It also helps us to see that we need a close relationship with each other as well as with Christ. We need to work together for the benefit of each other as well as to be the blessing to the world that God has called us to be. God has given each one of us opportunities, time, and talents to do this. And each one of us has an important function in developing essential Christian fellowship.

In order to work together we need the constant presence of the Holy Spirit in our lives. God freely gives the Holy Spirit to His children who ask. Jesus told us, "If you then, though you are evil, know how to give good gifts to your children, how much more will your Father in heaven give the Holy Spirit to those who ask him!" (Luke 11:13) The Holy Spirit guides us, teaches us, and gives us "love, joy, peace, patience, kindness, goodness, faithfulness, gentleness and self-control." (Galatians 5:22-23) All of these are qualities that each one of us needs in order to work together effectively.

The first and most important of these fruit of the Spirit is love. Loving each other is not only a good idea, it is commanded by Jesus. He said, "A new command I give you: Love one another. As I have loved you, so you must love one another. By this everyone will know that you are my disciples, if you love one another." (John 13:34-35) Jesus also taught that our love must reach out to more than our Christian fellowship. He said, "You have heard that it was said, 'Love your neighbor and hate your enemy.' But I tell you, love your enemies and pray for those who persecute you, that you may be children of your Father in heaven. He causes his sun to rise on the evil and the good, and sends rain on the righteous and the unrighteous. If you love those who love you, what reward will you get? Are not even the tax collectors doing that? And if you greet only your own people, what are you doing more than others? Do not even pagans do that? Be perfect, therefore, as your heavenly Father is perfect." (Matthew 5:43-48) [For more on living this life of love read first Corinthians chapter13 and chapter one of first John.]

True Christian fellowship can only exist between people who trust in Jesus as Savior and Lord. They believe that they will live with Jesus forever in heaven solely on the basis of what Jesus has done for them through His sacrificial death. They trust that what Jesus taught is the absolute truth for directing our lives. They love others, motivated by the love that God has already given them. Their associations with non-Christians are based on God's love that reaches out to all people. Their desire is to "live peaceful and quiet lives in all godliness and holiness, a life that pleases God their Savior, who wants all people to be saved and to come to a knowledge of the truth." (1Timothy 2:3-4) Christians especially avoid close associations with worldly people who draw them away from Christ in thoughts or deeds. That is why Paul warned the Corinthian Christians, "Do not be yoked together with unbelievers. For what do righteousness and wickedness have in common? Or what fellowship can light have with darkness?" (2Corinthians 6:14)

A Christian takes care of the physical body that God has given them. They recognize that it is a tool given to them to carry out the activities that God has prepared for them to accomplish. As Paul tells us, "Do you not know that your bodies are temples of the Holy Spirit, who is in you, whom you have received from God? You are not your own; you were bought at a price. Therefore honor God with your bodies." (1Corinthians 6:19-20) Rest, proper diet, and exercise are required to maintain the usefulness of our bodies as well as avoiding anything that is harmful to it.

We also read in second Corinthians, "What agreement is there between the temple of God and idols? For we are the temple of the living God. As God has said: 'I will live with them and walk among them, and I will be their God, and they will be my people.' Therefore, 'Come out from them and be separate, says the Lord. Touch no unclean thing, and I will receive you.' And, "I will be a Father to you, and you will be my sons and daughters, says the Lord Almighty.'" (2Corinthians 6:16-18) The primary meaning of the word "holy", as it is used in the Bible, means to be "set apart for a specific purpose or calling." As Christians, we have been set apart to be a holy people who are to be a blessing to others in words and in deeds. We are in the world but we are not worldly.

God's word also teaches that our individual temples are part of a greater temple which is also called the Body of Christ. God told us through Saint Paul, "Don't you know that you yourselves are God's temple and that God's Spirit dwells in your midst? If anyone destroys God's temple, God will destroy that person; for God's temple is sacred, and you together are that temple." (1Corinthians 3:16-17) Paul was led to elaborate on this analogy when he wrote, "Consequently, you are no longer foreigners and strangers, but fellow citizens with God's people and also members of his household, built on the foundation of the apostles and prophets, with Christ Jesus himself as the chief cornerstone. In him the whole building is joined together and rises to become a holy temple in the Lord. And in him you too are being built together to become a dwelling in which God lives by his Spirit." (Ephesians 2:19-22) Many materials and structural objects are needed to construct a building, some obvious and others hidden, but all are needed to build a structure that can serve effectively for the purpose it was built. God has a purpose and a particular place for each of us in His building.

Peter, whose name means rock, also uses this analogy of a temple for the image of Christian fellowship. He wrote, "As you come to him, the living Stone, rejected by humans but chosen by God and precious to him, you also, like living stones, are being built into a spiritual house to be a holy priesthood, offering spiritual sacrifices acceptable to God through Jesus Christ." (1Pter 2:4-5) And he elaborated on the reality and purpose of Christian fellowship when he wrote, "But you are a chosen people, a royal priesthood, a holy nation, God's special possession, that you may declare the praises of him who called you out of darkness into his wonderful light." (1Peter 2:9) What a magnificent depiction of each individual's importance and place in God's holy family!

God's Word compares Christian fellowship to a physical body, a temple in which God's Spirit lives, and also, more intimately, to a family. Matthew records that after healing a demon possessed man, "Jesus was still talking to the crowd, his mother and brothers stood outside, wanting to speak to him. Someone told him, Your mother and brothers are standing outside, wanting to speak to you." He replied to him, "'Who is my mother, and who are my brothers?' Pointing to his disciples, he said, 'Here are my mother and my brothers. For whoever does the will of my Father in heaven is my brother and sister and mother.'" (Matthew 12:46-50) Saint John gives us more insight into this familial relationship between God and Christians when he wrote, "Yet to all who did receive him, to those who believed in his name, he gave the right to become children of God, children born not of natural descent, nor of human decision or a husband's will, but born of God." (John 1:12-13) Through faith in Jesus Christ, trusting in Him alone for our present and eternal welfare, we are adopted by God into His family and loved as one of His own.

The writings of John emphasize the intimate association of love and fellowship between Christians. In the first of his three letters he wrote, "We proclaim to you what we have seen and heard, so that you also may have fellowship with us. And our fellowship is with the Father and with his

Son, Jesus Christ." (1John 1:3) John also depicts living in Christian fellowship as walking in the light of God's truth received from Jesus Christ. He wrote, ˝This is the message we have heard from him and declare to you: God is light; in him there is no darkness at all. If we claim to have fellowship with him and yet walk in the darkness, we lie and do not live out the truth. But if we walk in the light, as he is in the light, we have fellowship with one another, and the blood of Jesus, his Son, purifies us from all sin." (1John 1:5-7) When we walk in the light of Christ's wisdom and love, trusting Him and learning from Him through His Word, we grow personally, we grow in fellowship with each other, and we grow in fellowship with our Creator, Savior, and Guide.

Paul, in his letters, continually reminds us of the meaning and importance of Christian fellowship. To the Colossian Christians he wrote, "Let the peace of Christ rule in your hearts, since as members of one body you were called to peace. And be thankful." (Colossians 3:15) And to the Corinthian Christians, "God is faithful, who has called you into fellowship with his Son, Jesus Christ our Lord." (1Corinthians 1:9) And in benediction he writes, "May the grace of the Lord Jesus Christ, and the love of God, and the fellowship of the Holy Spirit be with you all." (2Corinthians 13:14)

My dear family and friends, REMAIN IN FELLOWSWHIP WITH GOD'S FAMILY.

SERVICE

Love in action

God gave us the Bible so that we would know that He loves us. He loved us so much that He sacrificed His only begotten Son to pay the penalty for our sins. By trusting in His Son we are adopted as God's children and are assured of an eternity with Him in heaven. The Bible, also, enables us to know how to live a blessed, joyful, fruitful life during our sojourn in time. God gave us the gift of prayer so that we might experience fellowship with Him. God draws us into the family of believers in order to have fellowship with each other, in order to use the gifts He gives each of His children, so that working together, we are able to be the Salt of the earth and the Light of the world, the blessing to the world that God has called us to be.

The Apostle Paul wrote about the Christian's response to God's grace in his letter to the Ephesian Christians: "For it is by grace you have been saved, through faith, and this is not from yourselves, it is the gift of God, not by works, so that no one can boast. For we are God's handiwork, created in Christ Jesus to do good works, which God prepared in advance for us to do." (Ephesians 2:8-10) Everyone who has been adopted into God's family has important work to do in bringing God's love to others.

Paul emphasized this again later in this same letter: "So Christ himself gave the apostles, the prophets, the evangelists, the pastors and teachers, to equip his people for works of service, so that the body of Christ may be built up until we all reach unity in the faith and in the knowledge of the Son of God and become mature, attaining to the whole measure of the fullness of Christ." (Ephesians 4:11-13) God chooses particular people that He uses to prepare the rest of us to bring His words and works of love to the people of the world.

The author of Hebrews points out that loving service is the natural result of Christians coming together. He writes, "Let us hold unswervingly to the hope we profess, for he who promised is faithful. And let us consider how we may spur one another on toward love and good deeds, not giving up meeting together, as some are in the habit of doing, but encouraging one another, and all the more as you see the Day approaching." (Hebrews 10:23-25) Every member of God's family has the responsibility of encouraging God's children to listen to their Father in heaven, to follow Jesus, and to be the world's blessing that God has called us to be.

Paul particularly praised the Macedonian Christians for their desire to be of service to some of their less fortunate brothers and sisters in the faith. He wrote, "And now, brothers and sisters, we want you to know about the grace that God has given the Macedonian churches. In the midst of a very severe trial, their overflowing joy and their extreme poverty welled up in rich generosity. For I testify that they gave as much as they were able, and even beyond their ability. Entirely on their own, they urgently pleaded with us for the privilege of sharing in this service to the Lord's people." (2Corinthians 8:1-4) No matter what our station in life might be, no matter what our earthly resources may be, God has a mission for each of us to fulfill and He will supply the motivation and the means to carry out that mission.

These Macedonian Christians were exemplifying the chief characteristic of the followers of Jesus Christ. As the Lord Jesus told His disciples, "A new command I give you: Love one another. As I have loved you, so you must love one another. By this everyone will know that you are my disciples, if you love one another." (John 13:34-35) The members of Jesus' family have an obligation to love their spiritual siblings so that they may more effectively work together to do the things that God has called them to do.

God tells us through both John and James that our love for others results in actions. John wrote, "This is how we know what love is: Jesus Christ laid down his life for us. And we ought to lay down our lives for our brothers and sisters. If anyone has material possessions and sees a brother or sister in need but has no pity on them, how can the love of God be in that person? Dear children, let us not love with words or speech but with actions and in truth." (1John 3:16-18) And from James we read, "What good is it, my brothers and sisters, if someone claims to have faith but has no deeds? Can such faith save them? Suppose a brother or a sister is without clothes and daily food. If one of you says to them, 'Go in peace; keep warm and well fed,' but does nothing about their physical needs, what good is it? In the same way, faith by itself, if it is not accompanied by action, is dead." (James 2:14-17) The faith of a child of God results in care for other members of the family as well as blessings for all people.

When people come to know the love that God has for them in Jesus Christ, they freely accept Him as Savior and Lord, and are anxious to follow Christ's commands. This is why the Apostle Paul could write, "You, my brothers and sisters, were called to be free. But do not use your freedom to indulge the flesh rather, serve one another humbly in love. For the entire law is fulfilled in keeping this one command: Love your neighbor as yourself." (Galatians 5:13-14) God's children show their love for Jesus and their heavenly Father by their loving actions directed toward God's creation, other people, and especially other members of the Family.

Once, upon hearing this, an expert in the law asked Jesus who his neighbor was. This was the occasion that Jesus used to tell the story of the Good Samaritan. While both a priest and a Levite ignored the fate of the traveler who was injured by robbers, a Samaritan took pity on him and went far out of his way to help him. Jesus then asked, " 'Which of these three do you think was a neighbor to the man who fell into the hands of robbers?' The expert in the law replied, 'The one who had mercy on him.'

Jesus told him, 'Go and do likewise.'" (Luke 10:36-37) Thus, Jesus made it clear that it is need of people that determines our decision to be of service to them, not their station in life.

Jesus made this quite clear in His Sermon on the Mount when He taught His hearers, "You have heard that it was said, 'Love your neighbor and hate your enemy.' But I tell you, love your enemies and pray for those who persecute you, that you may be children of your Father in heaven. He causes his sun to rise on the evil and the good, and sends rain on the righteous and the unrighteous. If you love those who love you, what reward will you get? Are not even the tax collectors doing that? And if you greet only your own people, what are you doing more than others? Do not even pagans do that? Be perfect, therefore, as your heavenly Father is perfect." (Matthew 5:43-48) Many organizations and societies in the world take care of their own people. But Christians recognize that their Father in heaven is the creator of all people and that they have been given the charge to be a blessing to all people, to be the Salt of the earth.

At first this may seem like a rather tall order - to care for everyone. But we must remember that we are called to care for our neighbor, those particular individuals and people that God brings near to our eyes and mind. We have the power of the One who fed five thousand with five loaves and two fish working with us. We are also working together with all of the Body of Christ, each using the resources, talents, and abilities that God has given. As Paul taught, "For just as each of us has one body with many members, and these members do not all have the same function, so in Christ we, though many, form one body, and each member belongs to all the others. We have different gifts, according to the grace given to each of us." (Romans 12:4-6) And again, "There are different kinds of gifts, but the same Spirit distributes them. There are different kinds of service, but the same Lord. There are different kinds of working, but in all of them and in everyone it is the same God at work." (1Corinthians 12:4-6) When we let God have complete control of our lives He gives us abilities and shapes our character to be perfectly suited for the part that He has called us to perform. Together, we work as His Family to be a blessing to all people and to bring glory to His Name.

Remember, you, together with all the members of God's

family, those who trust in Jesus as Lord and Savior, are the Salt of the earth. For Jesus told us, "You are the salt of the earth. But if the salt loses its saltiness, how can it be made salty again? It is no longer good for anything, except to be thrown out and trampled underfoot." (Matthew 5:13) You won't lose your saltiness if you continue to practice the first three Holy Habits - follow God's Word, seek His guidance and power through prayer, and remain in fellowship with other members of God's family.

The most beautiful thing about caring for others in obedience to Christ is that through doing this we are showing love for our Savior who has first loved us beyond measure. Jesus made this very clear in His depiction of the final judgment: "When the Son of Man comes in his glory, and all the angels with him, he will sit on his glorious throne. All the nations will be gathered before him, and he will separate the people one from another as a shepherd separates the sheep from the goats. He will put the sheep on his right and the goats on his left.

Then the King will say to those on his right, 'Come, you who are blessed by my Father; take your inheritance, the kingdom prepared for you since the creation of the world. For I was hungry and you gave me something to eat, I was thirsty and you gave me something to drink, I was a stranger and you invited me in, I needed clothes and you clothed me, I was sick and you looked after me, I was in prison and you came to visit me.'

Then the righteous will answer him, 'Lord, when did we see you hungry and feed you, or thirsty and give you something to drink? When did we see you a stranger and invite you in, or needing clothes and clothe you? When did we see you sick or in prison and go to visit you?'

The King will reply, 'Truly I tell you, whatever you did for one of the least of these brothers and sisters of mine, you did for me.'" (Matthew 25:31-40) We show love for Jesus by loving others.

Earthly leaders seek praise and honor from others. But Jesus is best served by serving those in need.

I believe that there are two things needed for happiness in life (1) to know that you are loved and (2) to know that you are able to love other people. God's love for us and His calling to serve as part of His family provide both of these needs.

My dear family and friends, SERVE OTHERS IN LOVE.

WITNESS

The Light of Truth

God's children have a beneficial purpose for life, they are to bring glory to their Father in heaven. They do this by proclaiming the wonderful works that He does in creation and and what He does for the people of the world, through His Son, and through His adopted children. Talking to others about God's amazing grace naturally follows from the service that God's people are called to do. Jesus was emphasizing this when He told His followers, "You are the light of the world. A town built on a hill cannot be hidden. Neither do people light a lamp and put it under a bowl. Instead they put it on its stand, and it gives light to everyone in the house. In the same way, let your light shine before others, that they may see your good deeds and glorify your Father in heaven." (Matthew 5:14-16) As God's children serve others they deflect the praise that they might receive toward Jesus and their heavenly Father. They want people to know who motivated them and directed their lives to serve others.

Christian service and Christian witness are inextricably bound together. Service without witness tends to bring glory to the ones who serve instead of to God who motivates and stirs the faithful toward service. Witness without service tends to lead toward an impression of hypocrisy toward those who witness. When the Christian community works together to serve and witness, to be Salt and Light, then the world is presented with a powerful presentation of God's grace.

There are people in the body of Christ who have been specifically gifted in the area of explaining the Good News of salvation through faith in Jesus Christ. We call them evangelists. They are one of the gifted people that Jesus has given to His church. As Paul wrote to the Ephesian Christians, "So Christ himself gave the apostles, the prophets, the evangelists, the pastors and teachers, to equip his people for works of service, so that the body of Christ may be built up until we all reach unity in the faith and in the knowledge of the Son of God and become mature, attaining to the whole measure of the fullness of Christ." (Ephesians 4:11-13) All Christians, however, need to be prepared to explain the faith that they have in Jesus when the opportunity arises. Saint Peter encourages all of us to do this in his first letter. He wrote, "But in your hearts revere Christ as Lord. Always be prepared to give an answer to everyone who asks you to give the reason for the hope that you have. But do this with gentleness and respect." (1Peter 3:15)

The early Christians provide an excellent example to us of a faithful witness. Following the execution of Stephen, the first Christian martyr, we learn of the amazingly beneficial effect of this persecution as the Christians were scattered. We read in the book of Acts, "On that day a great persecution broke out against the church in Jerusalem, and all except the apostles were scattered throughout Judea and Samaria. Godly men buried Stephen and mourned deeply for him. But Saul began to destroy the church. Going from house to house, he dragged off both men and women and put them in prison. Those who had been scattered preached the word wherever they went." (Acts 8:1-4) The apostolic leaders courageously remained in Jerusalem while the ordinary Christians told others about Jesus wherever they went.

And again in the book of Acts we read, "Now those who had been scattered by the persecution that broke out when Stephen was killed traveled as far as Phoenicia, Cyprus and Antioch, spreading the word only among Jews. Some of them, however, men from Cyprus and Cyrene, went to Antioch and began to speak to Greeks also, telling them the good news about the Lord Jesus. The Lord's hand was with them, and a great number of people believed and turned to the Lord." (Acts 11:19-21) All members of the Body of Christ have a part in bringing the Good News of Jesus Christ to the people of the world.

When the Israelites were about to enter the land that God had promised them, Moses, knowing that he would not be allowed to go with them, warned the children of Israel to pass on the experiences, recounting of miracles, and the laws that God had given them to their children and grandchildren. He said, "Only be careful, and watch yourselves closely so that you do not forget the things your eyes have seen or let them fade from your heart as long as you live. Teach them to your children and to their children after them." (Deuteronomy 4:9) God's children keep reminding each other, as well as other people, that God is at work to graciously bless all people, especially the members of His own family.

Paul also exhorted his readers to pass on the even greater message of the Gospel to their children. He wrote, "Fathers, do not exasperate your children; instead, bring them up in the training and instruction of the Lord." (Ephesians 6:4) This is why I am writing this message to you who are my children, grandchildren, and brothers and sisters in Christ. Before I am called home to be with Jesus, I want to be sure that you have received this ultimately important message from me.

It has been more than two thousand years since Jesus, the Son of God, took on our flesh and walked among us. God walked with Adam in the perfect world of the Garden of Eden. Jesus walked among us in this imperfect world to redeem us and to restore the world by sacrificing His perfect life for our imperfections. The first disciples were anxious to be part of that new world. After Christ's resurrection they came to Jesus with this anxious expectation. We read in Acts: "Then they gathered around him and asked him, 'Lord, are you at this time going to restore the kingdom to Israel?'

He said to them: 'It is not for you to know the times or dates the Father has set by his own authority. But you will receive power when the Holy Spirit comes on you; and you will be my witnesses in Jerusalem, and in all Judea and Samaria, and to the ends of the earth.'" (Acts 1:6-8)

We, also, do not need to know the times or dates that the Father has set. We simply need to use the time that He has given us here on earth to do the work that He has called us to do. God, who loves to give good gifts to His children, will give you the Holy Spirit for the asking. He will guide you into all the truth that you need to know to carry out the mission for which He has called you for this life. Your

"Jerusalem" may be your own family and relatives. Your "Judea and Samaria" may be at school or at work. For some of us our occupations may, indeed, bring us to the ends of the earth. And if God may call you to be an evangelist, you will be called to be supported by others to be the first to bring the Good News to a needy world.

The last five verses of the Gospel of Matthew are often referred to as "The Great Commission". It reads as follows: "Then the eleven disciples went to Galilee, to the mountain where Jesus had told them to go. When they saw him, they worshiped him; but some doubted. Then Jesus came to them and said, 'All authority in heaven and on earth has been given to me. Therefore go and make disciples of all nations, baptizing them in the name of the Father and of the Son and of the Holy Spirit, and teaching them to obey everything I have commanded you. And surely I am with you always, to the very end of the age.'" (Matthew 28:16-20) This commission is for all of God's people as they work together, using the gifts God has given them, in the position that God has placed them, to be the Salt of the earth and the Light of the world. I pray that you will consciously consider your part in the Great Commission and joyfully work with the rest of God's chosen people to be the blessing to the world that God has called us to be. May you, "Be dressed ready for service and keep your lamps burning." (Luke 12:35) May you truly be a part of the Salt and Light that Jesus calls us to be.

My dear family and friends, TELL OTHERS ABOUT JESUS.

CONCLUSION

Final thoughts

The post-resurrection occurrence that has particularly intrigued me over the years is the experience of the two travelers on the road to Emmaus. They were dejected, disillusioned, and without hope for the future when Jesus came to walk with them, teach them, and reveal His powerful presence to them. As He revealed Himself to them we read: "When he was at the table with them, he took bread, gave thanks, broke it and began to give it to them. Then their eyes were opened and they recognized him, and he disappeared from their sight. They asked each other, 'Were not our hearts burning within us while he talked with us on the road and opened the Scriptures to us?'" (Luke 24:30-32) When you have Jesus at the heart of your life, your heart, too, will burn with the fire of the Holy Spirit and your life will be blessed along with many others with whom your life interacts.

These Five Holy Habits that I have talked about in this letter are NOT Five Holy Disciplines. While discipline is necessary for an orderly life, discipline must be our servant, not our master. Every religion has some disciplines related to its beliefs. The Pharisees, who so vehemently opposed Jesus, were very disciplined in following the ceremonial laws of the Old Testament. The Law was their master. Their religion like all religions except Christianity was a religion of law. Christianity is not a religion of law, it is the only true religion of grace. Religion without grace only leads to pride and arrogance. Christians are humble people because they recognize the truth that they are sinful people and can never be worthy of heaven through their own disciplines of following God's laws. They believe that eternal life is a gift given to those who accept Jesus Christ as their Lord and Master.

Jesus warned us about the arrogance of a religion based on laws. He Said, "Be careful not to practice your righteousness in front of others to be seen by them. If you do, you will have no reward from your Father in heaven. So when you give to the needy, do not announce it with trumpets, as the hypocrites do in the synagogues and on the streets, to be honored by others. Truly I tell you, they have received their reward in full. But when you give to the needy, do not let your left hand know what your right hand is doing, so that your giving may be in secret. Then your Father, who sees what is done in secret, will reward you.

And when you pray, do not be like the hypocrites, for they love to pray standing in the synagogues and on the street corners to be seen by others. Truly I tell you, they have received their reward in full. But when you pray, go into your room, close the door and pray to your Father, who is unseen. Then your Father, who sees what is done in secret, will reward you." (Matthew 6:1-6)

Religions of law lead only to two destructive ends - pride

or despair. The proud person foolishly believes that he is worthy to stand before God on his own merits believing himself to be superior to other people. The despairing person wallows in hopelessness believing that there is no point in even trying to keep God's law. Yet, there is hope for both with Christ. He cuts out pride with a sharpened understanding of God's law and He wipes away despair with the soothing Gospel of God's grace.

The Five Holy Habits are a solid framework on which to hang all the rest of the teachings and practices of the Christian faith. They help us to make God's wonderful laws into a servant instead of our master. Our only Master is Jesus. Don't think that you are earning any favor with God by following the Five Holy Habits, you are doing yourself a favor. God's love for you is already infinite. God is pleased when He sees that His adopted children are wise enough to listen to Him and to conform themselves to the image of His only begotten Son.

According to Funk and Wagnalls 1976 Standard Desk Dictionary a habit is "an act or practice so frequently repeated as to become almost automatic." When the Five Holy Habits become an automatic part of the life of a Christian they provide the means to "grow in the grace and knowledge of our Lord and Savior Jesus Christ" (2Peter 3:18) They provide the basic pattern for following Jesus as one of His faithful disciples.

The primary function of the Christian church is to make disciples, to administer God's grace through the sacraments and to teach and preach God's Word. A disciple is basically a learner, according to its Greek meaning, and Jesus says, "Come to me, all you who are weary and burdened, and I will give you rest. Take my yoke upon you and learn from me, for I am gentle and humble in heart, and you will find rest for your souls. For my yoke is easy and my burden is light." (Matthew 11:28-30) When we practice the Five Holy Habits we are able to walk and learn from Jesus, not too differently than the original disciples.

The "easy and light" that Jesus was talking about does not mean that there will be no problems in life. What it means is that if you listen to Jesus, and live accordingly, you will have the wisdom and strength to know how to face the challenges that life will bring. Sometimes Christians may face difficulties in life simply because they are Christians. This might include ridicule, marginalization, persecution, or even loss of life. The devil, the world, and our own sinful desires are enemies that wage war against the souls of Christians. The elderly Apostle John wrote to Christians, "You, dear children, are from God and have overcome them, because the one who is in you is greater than the one who is in the world. They are from the world and therefore speak from the viewpoint of the world, and the world listens to them. We are from God, and whoever knows God listens to us; but whoever is not from God does not listen to us. This is how we recognize the Spirit of truth and the spirit of falsehood." (1John 4:4-6) Paul wrote to Timothy, "Fight the good fight of the faith. Take hold of the eternal life to which you were called when you made your good confession in the presence of many witnesses." (1Timothy 6:12)

And Jesus also said, "Enter through the narrow gate. For wide is the gate and broad is the road that leads to destruction, and many enter through it. But small is the gate and narrow the road that leads to life, and only a few find it." (Matthew 7:13-14) Luke wrote about various people who wanted to follow Christ without truly having Him as Lord of their life. He wrote: "As they were walking along the road, a man said to him, 'I will follow you wherever you go.'

Jesus replied, 'Foxes have dens and birds have nests, but the Son of Man has no place to lay his head.'

He said to another man, 'Follow me.'

But he replied, 'Lord, first let me go and bury my father.'

Jesus said to him, 'Let the dead bury their own dead, but you go and proclaim the kingdom of God.'

Still another said, 'I will follow you, Lord; but first let me go back and say goodbye to my family.'

Jesus replied, 'No one who puts a hand to the plow and looks back is fit for service in the kingdom of God.'" (Luke 9:57-62)

What it takes to truly follow Jesus is not a lot of self-determination, but faith in Jesus Christ. Faith that He died and rose that you could live with Him forever, faith that all His words are true, and faith that He will always keep His promises. As the author of Hebrews wrote, "And without faith it is impossible to please God, because anyone who comes to him must believe that he exists and that he rewards those who earnestly seek him." (Hebrews 11:6)

When Jesus calls us to follow Him through His Word, He calls us to a great responsibility. Nothing in life gives more satisfaction than to work hard at a task that is truly worthwhile. Nothing is more worthwhile than bringing the love of Jesus to people through words and actions. With faith in Jesus we can gladly accept the responsibility. As He tells us, "From everyone who has been given much, much will be demanded; and from the one who has been entrusted with much, much more will be asked." (Luke 12:48b)

I close this letter to you with some of my favorite words from Jesus, "As the Father has loved me, so have I loved you. Now remain in my love. If you keep my commands, you will remain in my love, just as I have kept my Father's commands and remain in his love. I have told you this so that my joy may be in you and that your joy may be complete. My command is this: Love each other as I have loved you. Greater love has no one than this: to lay down one's life for one's friends. You are my friends if you do what I command. I no longer call you servants, because a servant does not know his master's business. Instead, I have called you friends, for everything that I learned from my Father I have made known to you. You did not choose me, but I chose you and appointed you so that you might go and bear fruit, fruit that will last, and so that whatever you ask in my name the Father will give you. This is my command: Love each other." (John 15:9-17)

Jesus is the greatest GIFT of all.
Use His GIFT wisely - trust Him, obey Him.
Listen to Jesus by reading His Word.
Speak to Jesus in prayer.
Fellowship with Jesus, with His Family.
Serve Jesus by caring for those in need.
Give hope to others by telling them about Jesus.
God's grace and peace be with you.

With love,

Dad, Grandpa, Brother, Brother-in-law, Uncle, Friend

PS: "Do not store up for yourselves treasures on earth, where moths and vermin destroy, and where thieves break in and steal. But store up for yourselves treasures in heaven, where moths and vermin do not destroy, and where thieves do not break in and steal. For where your treasure is, there your heart will be also. (Matthew 6:19-21) "Keep your lives free from the love of money and be content with what you have, because God has said, 'Never will I leave you; never will I forsake you.'" (Hebrews 13:5)

"Remember your leaders, who spoke the word of God to you. Consider the outcome of their way of life and imitate their faith. Jesus Christ is the same yesterday and today and forever." (Hebrews 13:7-8)

LET'S TALK ABOUT THE FIVE HOLY HABITS

It All Starts With Jesus

Jesus is King above all kings and Lord above all lords. He is the Word of God, the Agent of creation.

He is one with God the Father and the only pathway into the presence of God. Anyone who wants to know about God needs to look to Jesus. He is the Anointed One, the Messiah. He is the Christ. That is why those who trust in Him are called **Christ**ians. That is why faith in Him is called **Christ**ianity. Its all about Jesus. Jesus made it clear that those who have faith in Him are His brothers and sisters and God is their Father. They are family. Christianity is not simply knowledge *about* Christ, but a relationship *with* Christ. Even the devil and demons know who Christ is. They don't believe in Him or want Him as Lord, yet He has supreme power over them. Christianity is a relationship more than a religion. It is not a set of rules to follow. It is a living dynamic relationship. It is family, a family that cuts across all divisions that men create. Anyone who is a member of the human race can be part of Christ's family.

It is a way of life, not a part of life. A person who trusts in Him as Savior will want to trust in Him as Lord of their life. Christians give control of their lives to the One who loves them more than any other. Christians trust in Jesus alone as Savior, the One who freely offered up His life as the atonement for the sins of the whole world.

Jesus knew that He would have to die like a seed planted in the ground. A seed that would sprout, that would be resurrected, that would produce a plant, a tree, a family tree, a living growing organism that is a blessing to the whole world. Christ's family tree continues to produce good fruit, the beneficial produce of people who listen to Jesus and put His words into practice in their lives. The same people who have eternal access to the tree of life.

Perhaps my favorite post-resurrection appearance of Jesus is when he walked with those two disciples on their way to Emmaus. Their hearts stirred with spiritual excitement as Jesus explained to them the Scriptures that pointed to Him as the suffering, resurrected, and conquering promised Christ. Walking with Christ through life is an exciting, yet peaceful, journey. Listening to Jesus, learning from Him through His Word, learning to think and act as a child of God, trusting in the love and good will of the Father - these are all a part of the Christian's walk with Jesus.

Trusting in Jesus makes a person a child of God. Faith in Him makes all the difference. We don't do activities like the five holy habits to become a child of God, we already are a child of God through faith in Jesus, the Son of God.

WHY FIVE HOLY HABITS?

The Five Holy Habits that are the heart of the Koinonia ministry were formulated to give the students of Concordia Lutheran High School in Fort Wayne, Indiana a practical Christian theology that would serve to direct their activities throughout their lifetime. They are the heart of "doing" Christianity. Jesus said that the people who "do" the will of His Father in heaven are part of His family, His brothers and sisters. The Five Holy Habits are activities that characterize the Christian life. Their focus is on the things that are the heart of what it means to be part of God's family. There is nothing sacred about the number. They are simply a way of clearly delineating the essential activities of a child of God. Doing the Five Holy Habits do not *make* you a child of God, you practice the Five Holy Habits because you *are* a child of God.

We call the Five Holy Habits "holy" because they characterize the activities of a holy people, people that God has set apart for His purposes. People do not make themselves holy, God makes them holy through faith in His only begotten Son. Christians are holy because God has called them and set them apart for His purposes. Christians are holy because they have given over control of their lives to an all-powerful, all-knowing, always present, all-loving God that they can call "Father" through faith in Jesus Christ. The Bible calls all Christians saints. They are a "holy people" called by God to be Salt and Light for the world. They are called to be a blessing to the world through their loving actions and through their faithful witness to the love of the heavenly Father who gave His Son up to be the Lamb of God whose sacrifice on the cross paid for the sin of the whole world.

The children of Israel were not allowed to approach God at Mount Sinai because God was protecting them from His holy presence. Sin and sinful people cannot exist in the presence of our holy God. Only people who have been made holy by God are allowed into His presence and they are only made holy through faith in Jesus Christ. Jesus is the prophet that God told Moses about, the prophet to whom the people must listen. It is only through faith in Jesus, through trusting Him as Savior and Lord, that anyone can come near to God. They are even invited into God's presence like children playing in the palace of the King. God's call to faith in His Son goes out to every human being; and those who believe are purified, justified, and sanctified (set apart) by God.

Why habits as opposed to disciplines? Habits are activities that a person does because of who they are. Disciplines are activities that a person does in order to achieve something, in order to become a certain kind of person. It is the difference between law and grace. It is only through God's grace that anyone can be a child of God, to be part of His family, to be a member of the family tree. And just as a good tree bears good fruit, God's children bear good fruit because of who they are, not because of who or what they want to become.

God takes ordinary things and makes them special. We see this in Christ's institution of holy communion. The elements are common bread and wine, not cake and champagne. This is characteristic of how God acts in and with humanity. He takes ordinary human beings and makes them into His children. This has profound theological significance for Christians and for the whole world. Christians follow God's way of doing things. They trust God's Word for every decision in life – not emotion – not human logic – not short term help with bad long term consequences. They seek God's guidance through His Word for ordinary, every day activities, like a tree that grows quietly, almost imperceptibly, patiently growing leaves that absorb energy from the sun (Son), enabling it to draw up water and nutrients from below, in order to produce fruit that is pleasant to the eye and nourishing to the body

WHY SCRIPTURE?

I am a product of the Reformation with its three great *solas.* I came to trust in Jesus through the witness of Matthew, Mark, Luke, John, Paul and the other inspired writers of God's word. An honest look at my own sinful nature clearly showed me that I needed to trust in something, Someone, beyond myself for truth and guidance in this life. In the Bible I came to know the one true God who loved me more than any other person. Here God's grace took hold of me, surrounded me, protected me, and gave me direction. My faith in Jesus came by God's Spirit acting through God's Word.

Sola gratia and *sola fide* can only be comprehended through *sola scriptura,* yet the three are dependent on each other. God's grace gives us faith to believe and trust God's Word. Faith in God's grace comes through God's Word. God's Word works Faith in us to accept God's grace.

All messages from pastors and preachers must flow from God's word. Error comes in when anyone seeks to verify their own ideas by picking and choosing from God's Word. Even Satan knows God's Word, but he twists it into something that deceives and destroys. The only reliable source for guidance for this life and the next is *sola scriptura.* It is

God's message to us and for us. The pronouncements of all Christians must be held up against the infallible Scriptures before they can be accepted as acceptable for thoughts and actions. The ideas of men, divorced from God's Word, are always tainted with imperfection. All Christians need to follow the example of the Berean Jews who tested what Paul was telling them against the sacred Scriptures.

A person cannot approach an all-powerful, all-knowing, holy God in a way that seems right to any human being. He must approach God in a way that God Himself has provided. The children of Israel before Mount Sinai as well as the people who built the tower of Babble bear witness to that. Christian cults have their own skewed translations of God's word. They may also put forth secondary works that add to the Scriptures or take away from them. All through the Bible we see God taking the initiative to choose and come to men. The incarnation of Jesus Christ is the ultimate example of this pattern

For nearly four thousand years God has been choosing certain men to transmit His Word to mankind. A little over two thousand years ago God came Himself as a man – the God-man Jesus Christ. His life and death and resurrection opened the pathway for mankind to approach God's throne of grace. His inspired followers also left us an account of the message He came to give us and the example of how to live life as a child of God. The thirty-nine books of the inspired Word of God are a great gift that God has given us that enables us to know both Him and our relationship to Him.

For the Christian, then, the study and meditation on God's Word that He has revealed to us in the Bible is the means that He has given for us to know Him and to know who we are as a part of His creation. Christians need God's Word in their heart language so that they can better know God, to better know God's call into His family, and to better know their calling and place within God's family. Many Christian organizations are working to provide God's Word to all the people of the world in their native languages. They are seeking to provide accurate and understandable translations from the original languages so that every person can encounter God through the messages He has given us.

The ability and opportunity to study God's Word for ourselves is a prerequisite for becoming a Berean-like Christian. The application of God's Word to our lives is the heart of Christian living and personal Bible study is great preparation for effective Christian fellowship. Interactive Bible study, sharing the insights that the Holy Spirit gives us, directs the actions that we are to take as a family, working together to be the Salt and Light that God has called us to be. God's Word compares itself to a very sharp instrument, a two-edged sword. Using our continuing analogy, we might say that Scripture prunes the family tree getting rid of fruitless branches and directing the new growth toward the sun (Son) preparing those branches to produce good fruit.

WHY PRAYER?

God invites us to listen to Him through His Word. He also invites us to talk to Him through the medium of our prayers. Jesus taught His disciples to pray to God as their Father. Prayer for the Christian is much more than a command or a pleading session with a not too caring god. Prayer for the Christian is a gift that is a wonderful part of a relationship with a loving God. Only Christians can have this intimate relationship to God as Father since Jesus is the only avenue for access to God as Father.

When the disciples asked Jesus to teach them to pray, He began that prayer with the pronoun "our" showing that prayer to God the Father also implies a familial relationship with other Christians. For this reason many Christian denominations include the joint recitation of the Lord's prayer as a part of their worship services.

Private prayer is also considered by Jesus in His teaching. He encouraged private prayer as opposed to public prayers that are ostentatiously offered as a display of public piety. Jesus is not opposed to individuals speaking prayers for gathered Christians. As always He is concerned for the inner condition of the heart because real fellowship with God happens internally for each individual Christian. When members of a

Christian fellowship focus on the words of a prayer leader they are able to agree with an "Amen" in their thoughts.

Private prayer that occurs within the confines of one's own room or one's own thoughts is a particularly intimate encounter with our loving Father God. Jesus emphasized that the heavenly Father hears and rewards such private prayer. When the child of God, asks, seeks, and knocks in prayer, believing that his heavenly Father loves to give good things to His children, there is an intimate relationship between God the Father and His child that transcends all others.

When Christians consciously acknowledge their calling to serve others and to be a witness to God's love and goodness, they consistently seek God's direction through prayer and the study of God's Word. They seek the guidance of the Holy Spirit to direct their thoughts and actions. Prayer is an essential part of preparing for action associated with the life of a child of God. They freely offer themselves as instruments through whom God blesses even those who do not believe in Him or follow Him.

Prayer is an essential part of our fellowship with God. People who care about each other take time to communicate with each other. God talks to His children through His Spirit filled Word and His children speak to Him through their prayers and praises. Children in a loving family freely ask for things that they need or want. They also accept the loving correction of their parents. They come to their parents for help, comfort, affection, and direction. While God is honored when His children come to Him with their praises, He is also honored when they come to Him with their petitions, recognizing that all good things come from Him. The prayer of a child of God is more than making requests to God it may includes confession, praise of their heavenly Father, thanking Him for His many blessings, and expressions of confidence in His blessings, guidance, and love.

Some have suggested that a formula for prayer might be expressed by the acronym ACTS, Adoration, Confession, Thanksgiving, and Supplication. Through adoration God's all-encompassing attributes, omnipotence, omniscience, omnipresence, graciousness, mercy, and love are acknowledged. Through confession and the acceptance of God's forgiveness the children of God get rid of the burden of sin that weighs on them physically and psychologically, keeping them from effective service and witnessing. Through thanksgiving God is honored as the giver of all of our gifts, all of our opportunities, and the fellowship of the members of our loving spiritual family. Through supplication God is honored as the great giver of every blessing, for this life and the next. It honors God when we ask of Him. He loves to give good things to His children

While such a thing as the ACTS pattern for prayer is helpful in formulating words to express our thoughts. God's children know that He even knows and acknowledges the unexpressed innermost feelings that defy any formulation into words. God is the ultimate Father figure who carefully watches over the growth and welfare of His children.

Prayer is the fluid that flows up and down the inner pathways of the Family tree. It carries the nutrients that are drawn up with the water of baptism from below. It flows to the leaves where it is transformed into nutrients that produce the fruit of the Spirit. It flows throughout the tree giving it the structure, strength, and nourishment that it needs.

WHY FELLOWSHIP?

God did not create people to be isolated individuals. We need each other. We need the loving touch of a parent, a spouse, a child. The Bible calls fellow believers brothers and sisters. Jesus called His disciples friends. Christian fellowship is like a family gathered around Jesus, listening to what He teaches them. It is much more than a club where people who have some common interest come together. There is such a strong intimate connection between the members of God's family that Scripture calls the gathered believers "the body of Christ."

When we are called into fellowship with Jesus Christ we are called into the "family business", the business of bringing God's love in Jesus Christ to the world through words and deeds. This is an awesome task and we need many different abilities to carry out our mission. No one person has anything close to all the gifts needed to carry out this mission. We recognize the gifts that God has given to each person in God's family and we value them as brothers and sisters and members of the body of Christ.

As family members we have two responsibilities – to encourage each other to use our talents and abilities to their fullest and to hold each other accountable for carrying out our family responsibilities. Unlike Cain, we are our brother's (and sister's) keepers. Christians pray for each other. They lovingly correct each other based on God's Word. They study God's Word together, seek His will together, and comfort each other in times of loss, sickness, or discouragement.

The loving fellowship of believers is characteristic of Christ's family. Within this loving circle they seek God's will for each other and support each other. That love wells up within the body of believers and naturally overflows to the people who are outside of the family. It is how the world perceives the followers of Jesus. The love that Christians have for each other prepares them to work together to love people who are not in the family.

As Christians study God's Word individually they are preparing to interact around God's Word in small interactive gatherings of Family members. In effect, they are walking with Jesus as they interact around His Word and use it to help each other to gain information, to find inspirations, to obtain guidance, to secure confirmation, and to focus on a direction individually and collectively to carry out Christ's commands to love God, to love each other, and to reach out with truth and love to the world around them. In small group interactive Bible study they walk with Jesus, listen to the Spirit, and experience the love of the Father.

Isolated Christians are not effective in carrying out the work that Christ has called them to do. Each of us has God-given gifts but none of us has every gift. We find completeness in fellowship with each other. We can see God working in each other when we come together and work together in loving fellowship. Our love for our Christian brothers and sisters empowers and enhances our love for others.

Jesus gave us His model for a working fellowship when He sent out His disciples in pairs. He gave them their mission and gave them special gifts and sent them out into the waiting harvest.

All parts of the Family Tree need each other in order to produce fruit. The branches must be firmly attached to the sturdy trunk (Jesus) in order to transport the life-giving sap out to the twigs and eventually to the leaves and growing fruit. Fruit offered freely for all to take.

WHY SERVICE?

God chose the prophet Abraham to be the ancestor of a great nation through whom all nations on the earth would be blessed. God blessed the whole world by sending Christ into the world as a descendant of Abraham. God loved the people that He created so much that He sent His only begotten Son into the world as a descendant of Abraham to redeem the people He created. Believers in Jesus Christ are the spiritual descendants of Abraham through whom God continues to bless the world. They bring God's blessings to the world through their actions and through their words of witness to God's love and grace.

By washing the feet of His chosen ones, Jesus made it clear to His inner circle that in order to care for the people of the world they must first care for each other. Following Jesus' example, service to the world starts with Christ's family. Their loving acts toward each other, that Jesus commanded as a characteristic of His followers, is a model for all humanity. Loving each other and loving those outside of the Family opens up doors for witnessing and draws people into the Family.

Loving others is the Family business and the members of Christ's Family recognize that all their time, talents, and treasure comes from God and are to be used to bless others, both within the Family and without. The greatest resource that God's children have, however, is the presence and guidance of the Holy Spirit, the Comforter and Paraclete who is always present at Family gatherings. As God works through His Family members to bless others, it gives them a sense of worth, it confirms their place in God's family giving them a sense of belonging. Working together also increases their appreciation of each other and strengthens the bonds that hold them together.

Jesus gave the model for the Family business during His ministry. While His primary mission was to seek and to save lost humanity, He taught and demonstrated how to live as a child of God. Along with the blessing of His teaching He blessed people through His actions. He healed the deaf, blind, sick and lame and ejected demons that were destroying the lives of the people that they inhabited. Likewise, works of healing accompanied those that Jesus sent out. In the same way, works of service are to take place wherever Jesus sends members of his Family. The wonderful message of the Gospel of God's love for mankind must be accompanied by loving service activities.

Jesus called His followers "the Salt of the earth." Just as salt is both used as a flavoring and a preservative, it is the loving actions of Christ's followers that add good flavor to life so that people may experience the goodness of God's love and receive the preservative that prevents life from becoming rotten. Jesus also characterized the kingdom that He rules as leaven that is hidden in a large lump of dough. People may not perceive Christ's kingdom but they can perceive that life is better where Christians are living according to the pattern that Jesus gave.

The *agape* love that Jesus commands His Family members to give to others is more than well wishes or emotions. It is love that shows itself through loving actions. Just as God's love for mankind can be seen through the actions of sending and sacrificing His Son, the love that Christians give to their neighbors is seen through loving actions. In a sense, when Christians give of their time and treasure to bless others, they are exchanging their earthly blessings for heavenly treasure. They are certain that they are not earning heaven because of their actions, and they are equally certain that they are storing up treasure in heaven that nothing can remove or destroy. They know that the best way that they can show their love for Christ is through the loving actions that they extend to others

At the Creation God placed Adam in the Garden of Eden to work and to take care of it. God wants His children to be responsible stewards of what He has given them. Jesus, also, wants His followers to produce fruit. He wants them to yield a fruitful harvest, a harvest of souls. He is looking for an increase, an increase of faith, hope, and love as His people interact with each other, and in turn as they interact with people of the world. While the blossoms (worship services) on a fruit tree may be beautiful to behold, they are utterly useless if they don't eventually lead to producing fruit, the fruit of the Spirit that Paul wrote about in chapter five of his letter to the Galatian Christians.

WHY WITNESS?

As children of God our ultimate purpose is to increase the size of the Family. We want everyone to come to know the great love that our Father in heaven has for all people. We dare not give the impression that we, ourselves, are the source of the love that causes us to care for others. We want them to come to know Jesus Christ as the motivator for our loving actions. Indeed, in His sermon on the mount Jesus said that we should let our light, our witness, shine forth in such a way that God the Father gets the glory and the credit. When those who are helped by our loving actions give us thanks, we have a great opportunity to point to Jesus as the ultimate source for Christian care and the great Redeemer that God sent for all people of the world.

In our fellowship with other Christians we not only encourage each other to use the gifts God has given us to bless others but we also prepare ourselves to give a clear witness to God's love for all people through the teaching, life, death, and resurrection of our Savior. As God's children we want all people to come to know God as the ever-living head of our Family and Jesus Christ as our Savior and Lord.

The greatest blessing we can give people is to introduce them to Jesus, the only-begotten Son of God and the redeemer of mankind. Our own activities are a means through which God works. They are simply the way to point people to the true source of love, to point them to the God who is love.

The Christian witness is all about the Gospel, God's love for mankind assured through the life, and death, and resurrection of God's Son as the full payment for the sins of mankind. It is the message of the incarnation; it is God putting on human flesh and sacrificing himself for the sins of the whole world; it is lifting Jesus up as the only, yet sure, hope of eternal life.

Jesus calls the members of His family "The Light of the world" Collectively they work together to bring the truth to a darkened world. All God's children are called to bear witness to the truth, to lift up Jesus to the world. He is truth itself, He is the only way to heaven, and He is the source of present and eternal life.

When Jesus met the eleven disciples on that mountain in Galilee He commissioned them to make disciples wherever they went. That commission continues to be the mission of the Children of God to the end of time. The dispensing of God's grace through baptism and the teaching of Christ's commands are the means. The Five Holy Habits are simply a practical way to teaching new disciples to follow their Savior and Lord as a child of God.

Witnessing is the flower that adorns the Family fruit Tree. It is the sweet message of the Gospel of Jesus Christ, the message that attracts repentant sinners, the soothing message that gives peace to the soul and a sure hope of eternal life. Those flowers of fruit trees are the promise of fruit to follow, fruit that bears the seeds that produce more trees, more groups of believers in Jesus Christ, and more loving actions as God works through more and more of His adopted children to bless the world. And all during the life of the Tree the Spirit, the life-giving wind from God, flows into the tree with nourishment, and out again with life-sustaining air.

IN CONCLUSION

In the conclusion to Christ's sermon on the mount as recorded by Matthew, Jesus spoke of two houses, one built on sand and the other on solid rock. It is the story of two different persons, one foolish and the other wise. The wise builder built on the Rock; he listened to Jesus and put His words into practice.

They are words for living life as a member of God's family. Jesus is not talking about how to get to heaven, how to make God love you, or how to be important in the eyes of other people. Jesus is talking about how to live as a child of God, how to weather the storms of the devil, the world, and our own sinful desires, how to live a fruitful life that is a blessing to oneself and others.

The Five Holy Habits are not what people do to become a Christian, they are what people do because they are Christians. The Five Holy Habits are simply faith in action. They don't require our intellectual analysis. They are the common life activities of the Children of God.

In summary, the Five Holy Habits are:

Scripture – the guide for living for those who will be eternally living with Jesus

Prayer – daily interaction with the Father, Jesus, and the Spirit

Fellowship – daily living with our brothers and sisters in Christ

Service – working together in the family business of blessing others.

Witness – letting people know of the peace and joy and eternal security that comes from following Jesus.

The author's prayer for you, the reader of this book, is that you will listen to Jesus, put His words into practice in your life, and be blessed by walking with Jesus and the rest of His Family through this life and on into a glorious eternity.

THE FIVE HOLY HABITS AND
THE KOINONIA MINISTRY

This section of this book is intended for Christian educators, particularly those who work in a Christian High School. It will explain in more detail how the Five Holy Habits were developed and their relationship to the Koinonia Ministry at Concordia Lutheran High School (CLHS) in Fort Wayne, Indiana. "Koinonia" is the biblical word for "fellowship". The name Koinonia was chosen for the name of the ministry because it describes the ministry that CLHS introduced to help us develop Christian leadership skills in our students. After reading this section, anyone who is interested in developing a similar program at their high school may contact me at HUSHAI@JUNO.COM.

Factors that led us to Koinonia

The mission statement of our high school is "Concordia Lutheran High School pursues Christ-centered educational excellence that equips individuals for lifelong learning and service as disciples of Jesus Christ." We believe that excellent Christian education must be directed toward preparing our graduates to live in a world that often ignores Jesus Christ or may even be hostile to Him and His teachings. Therefore, Christian education must not only present the faith as a system of beliefs but as a way of life lived in fellowship with other believers in Jesus Christ, a fellowship of Christians working to be what God has called, sanctified, and empowered them to be, the Salt of the earth and the Light of the world.

Our mission statement and the Koinonia ministry grew out of our meetings to prepare for our periodic accreditation visitations. During the 2001 - 2002 school year the faculty and administration began our school improvement discussions for the visitation by North Central, the State of Indiana, and the Lutheran School Association. The first consideration was an examination of the school's philosophy and mission statement. This involved the participation of the entire community connected with CLHS. Surveys were given to the constituents of CLHS. Separate questionnaires were given to the faculty, parents, students, and alumni to obtain their views of the adequacy of the educational practices, administrative policies, and supporting programs of the school. The faculty also met in small groups early in the school year to discuss the mission of the school.

Midway through the school year, after reviewing the wealth of data that was obtained, the faculty narrowed the focus for the school improvement plan to two goal areas: academic and faith life. The faith life goal was focused on putting faith into action. It was to be designed to develop Christian leadership skills that put what was taught in the religion classroom into action. It was to encompass everyone who was connected with the daily operation of CLHS – students, teachers, and support staff.

Our goal was to develop within the students the desire to practice living the Christian faith, to go beyond head knowledge to heart knowledge. We wanted them to practice living in a Christian community where people work for each other and with each other. We wanted to develop Christian leaders, people who can articulate the faith as well as demonstrate it. We believe that relationships grow and develop in small groups. Large gatherings of Christians are essentially built up of smaller groups in which growth can take place in a comfortable and caring environment. Our model was demonstrated by Jesus himself. While Jesus talked to the crowds, He also developed a much more intimate teaching relationship with the Twelve as He was preparing them to be the Apostles that He called them to be..

Rather than trying to build a totally new program, it was decided to contact the other Lutheran high schools in the United States to see if they might have programs that might be similar to what we were looking for. Mark Dolde (to whom this book is dedicated) and I contacted all the Lutheran high schools through letters and emails asking for information about any programs that they might already have in place that we might consider. One high school in particular, Saint Louis Lutheran High School South, had a program that had been operating for several years that looked particularly promising. Rev. Ron Roma had developed the program with the aid of area Directors of Christian Education and youth ministers. It was a small group, student led program with adults present to monitor and participate in the activities, devotions, and prayers. There were approximately eighteen students in each of their groups. Upon presenting these findings to the mentoring committee it was decided to investigate their program more fully.

After consulting with Rev. Roma the committee encouraged the development of a program similar to that at the St. Louis high school. It was decided that the best approach for us to teach Christian leadership skills to our students was to actually have them lead a small group of their own. The student body of the school was to be divided into groups of about twelves students each. These twelve consisted of three from each of the senior, junior, sophomore, and senior classes. The students in the same class would then stay with their group during their years at Concordia High School. The student leaders would be taken from the junior and senior classes with sophomores acting as assistant leaders.

Each Koinonia leader was to have an adult mentor who would work with the leader, outside of the Koinonia meeting time, to assist the leader to evaluate how they were doing as a leader, to encourage them, and to help them to develop greater leadership skills. During the Koinonia meeting the mentor would simply be another member of the group. The overall Koinonia ministry would have a faculty coordinator who would organize the groups, meet weekly with the Koinonia leaders as a group, and work with the adult mentors to increase their effectiveness. The faculty and staff would also be organized into their own small groups, called Unity Fellowship Groups UFG's), to study God's word together, to pray for each other, to share mentoring ideas with each other, and to encourage each other.

Development of the Koinonia Ministry

When developing the Koinonia ministry we envisioned the establishment of Koinonia Groups that would meet once during each week as a regular part of the schedule according to the following model: They were to:

1. provide a forum for adult-student interactions in a setting more relaxed than the traditional classroom
2. provide an opportunity for student-student interactions spanning traditional grade-level barriers.
3. provide an opportunity for students to discuss issues of concern to them in a non-threatening and non-judgmental environment.
4. give students an opportunity to develop and use spiritual leadership gifts.
5. give adults and students a chance to share with, encourage and support each other during troublesome times.
6. provide an opportunity for display of positive student and adult role models.
7. provide an opportunity to search the Scriptures for answers to problems and questions.
8. provide a small group environment in which prayers and intercessions can be made for each other, for our school, for our church, for our community, for our nation, and for our world.
9. address issues of particular importance to the students.

The following concerns were also addressed:

1. How can we be proactive and address the problems of watering down the theological position of CLHS?
   a. Do we have a statement of the theological position of CLHS from which to address this issue?
   b. We need to identify the issues that will be sensitive so that they may be addressed in the class. The adult partners need to be made aware of these particular issues so that they may work with the student leader to address the issue
2. How can we address situations that arise with respect to doctrine and theology?
   a. A workshop should be conducted for the adult leaders that anticipate these sensitive areas including how to deal with these issues if they arise.
   b. The workshop should result in a handbook that might be consulted when these issues arise.
3. Are there ways and things we can do to prepare for the eventuality of calming the constituency? [for discomfort related to something new]
   a. Invite them in to look at the program and then listen to them.
   b. Emphasize the faith-into-action goal of the program. (Hebrews 10:24)
4. How much thought will be given to the adult-student pairings?

      a. The adults and students will be carefully paired with each other. We saw this as critical.

      b. Adults will have some input as to the student leader that they feel they could mentor best.

5. Support groups should be considered for the faculty-student leader teams.

      a. This will be an important function of our Unity Fellowship Groups.

      b. Frequent communication of successes, solutions, and suggestions through e-mail can help.

6. We need to clarify the emphasis for the Koinonia groups.

      a. Our surveys that led to this program clearly indicated that the emphasis should be faith in action, walking in the light, exhibiting the fruit of the Spirit, walking the talk, practical, everyday, faith living.

      b. In order to do "a" we absolutely must encourage a closer walk with Jesus, listening to Him, having Him truly 'at the center', having Jesus as Lord.

7. How can we help the teachers with the perceived change in direction?

      a. We need to remind them of what the surveys indicated.

      b. The only real change has been from teacher directed groups to student mentored leader groups. This change was made after evaluating successful programs in other Lutheran high schools.

   c. The student led direction also alleviates the problem of another teacher preparation.

   d. The student led format also offers great opportunities for training future church leaders.

   e. We need to remind each other of the mission of CLHS.

Starting Out

To get the ministry started the faculty and administration chose me as the Koinonia coordinator and Mark Dolde as my assistant. To begin the Koinonia ministry we needed to identify potential student leaders who had both the spiritual and social skills we felt were necessary. Both students and staff were asked to nominate such individuals. Following is the form that was distributed to students and faculty members:

> In order to enhance the spiritual growth opportunities at CLHS, small groups, that we call Koinonia Groups, will be organized for the next school year. Koinonia is the Greek word for fellowship. In these groups we are seeking guidance for the issues that confront us as individuals, as a Christian high school, as a nation, and as part of God's creation.

> This week we will be seeking nominations for student leaders for the Koinonia Groups from next year's junior and senior classes.

Also, next year's sophomores may be nominated for assistant leader positions. All students and faculty at CLHS are encouraged to nominate students for these leadership positions. From the completed applications the student leaders will be chosen by a faculty committee. The identification of these students is critical to the effectiveness of our mentoring program.

The qualities we are looking for in our student leaders are:

1. They demonstrate the fruit of the Spirit in their lives
2. Others will listen to them
3. They are a positive role model in and outside of school
4. They have a strong Christian background
5. They have strong convictions, but are not overpowering
6. They work and play well with others

Each person who was nominated received a form letter telling them that they had been nominated along with an application form containing the following four questions:

1. State two or three reasons why you feel that you may be able to serve effectively as a Koinonia Group leader.
2. What spiritual gifts do you feel you have that are necessary to be an interactive Biblical discussion leader?

3. Give an example of how you work well with both adults and teenagers.

4. Most importantly, what effect does your faith in Jesus Christ have on your life?

In addition to identifying leaders for the Koinonia ministry we wanted all the constituencies connected with Concordia High School to be informed and to pray for the implementation of the Koinonia ministry. We, therefore, prepared a brief description of the ministry to be presented in all appropriate venues. This statement follows:

> Christian education must always be more than simply the education of Christians. One important thing that ought to happen whenever Christians come together is that they stir each other up for love and good works. (Hebrews 10:24) Education by itself is neither good nor bad, it is only one important factor that increases the capacity of the individual for accomplishing either good or evil. Whether good or bad comes as a result of the education of any person depends on the character of that person. The Koinonia Groups encourage the development of Christian character traits within the members of the group that encourage the utilization of God-given abilities, skills, and education for loving actions and a faithful Christian witness.

Good Christian education takes place when both students and teachers understand the struggle that always takes place between the flesh and the spirit as long as we are in this world. We must maintain constant contact with God's Word if we are to know who our real enemy is and what resources we have for fighting the good fight. Through the Holy Scriptures we know how much God loves us, we learn to keep our priorities in the proper order, and we develop that atmosphere of repentance and forgiveness that binds us together as one body in Christ. Within the Koinonia groups the guidance of the Holy Spirit is sought to lead us to put the truths of Scripture into practice in our lives

Following the example of the Berean Christians (Acts 17:10-12), God's Word is valued as the ultimate authority for directing our lives. Koinonia Groups are characterized by prayer and meditative study of the Scriptures directed towards following Christ as Savior and Lord. Real life issues will be studied and discussed seeking Biblical perspectives with the desire to let these principles direct our lives.

The Concordia Lutheran High School Koinonia Ministry is a combined effort of both students and staff doing ministry as a team. The greatest strength in our school is that we focus everything on the love and grace of our Lord Jesus Christ. Through prayer and God's word we seek answers to the challenges, and situations that confront youth as they live out their faith in our society.

Trusting in Jesus' promise that He is present where two or three are gathered together in His Name, we are confident that these times together will improve our faith walk. We also trust that God will give His Holy Spirit to His children who ask. As we pray together and meditate on God's word the Spirit will guide us and stir up our hearts for living with Jesus as Lord.

In addition to this statement a series of questions and answers were prepared to answer further questions that people, and students in particular, might have concerning this new ministry.

<u>Frequently Asked Questions About the Koinonia Groups</u>

1. What does KOINONIA mean? This is a Greek word used 20 times in the New Testament referring to the fellowship of the early Christians. It is an association of fellow-believers into a community characterized by joint participation. It is exemplified in Acts 2:42.

2. What is the purpose of the Koinonia Groups? The Koinonia Groups and Unity Fellowship Groups are the means by which we will meet the need the faculty of CLHS identified during the 2001-2002 school year for a spiritual mentoring program for all members of the CLHS family. This is the first goal of our current school improvement program.

3. What is a mentor? In the Odyssey Mentor was the sage guardian that Odysseus appointed for Telemachus. The title 'mentor' has come to mean a wise and trusted adviser, a friend, and teacher. Jesus is the ultimate mentor for Christians.

4. Do we have a vision for what the Koinonia Groups will be? Yes, and the vision will continue to become more clear as we search the Scriptures together and pray for the guidance of the Holy Spirit. The Koinonia Groups are to be a caring, interactive fellowship of students and adult mentors for the purpose of preparing the students and enabling all of us for life-long learning as disciples of Jesus Christ. They are to be communities of fellow believers, gathered in prayer around God's Word seeking the guidance of the Holy Spirit for the problems and issues that confront us in the present, or may confront us in the future. We will seek to stir each other up for love and good deeds (Hebrews 10:23-25) and to put Christ's teachings into practice in our lives (John 8:31-32).

5. When will the Koinonia Groups meet? There will be a special Koinonia day schedule similar to a

chapel day schedule. They will meet once per week for approximately one half hour.

6. Will the Unity Fellowship Groups continue to meet? Yes, we will continue to meet in prayer and meditation on the Scriptures. These meetings will also provide us with a means to encourage and support each other as we mentor our students. At these times we can share ideas with each other that may enable each of us to be more effective in our ministrations.

7. Will there be preparation time for the leaders? The Unity Fellowship Groups are to help us prepare to mentor our students. It will be the responsibility of the Spiritual Life Coordinator to prepare lists of Scripture references and notes for all students and adults to use as they seek guidance for the issues they are considering in their Koinonia Groups. The adult leaders will serve to direct the discussions along Scriptural guidelines and may offer their prayerful insight when appropriate.

8. Will there be student leaders in each Koinonia Group? An attempt will be made to get a good mix of students in each group based on both age and spiritual maturity. It is hoped that eventually each Koinonia Group can be occasionally divided into smaller student led groups. This is in line with our mission to prepare our students for life-long learning as disciples of Jesus Christ.

9. What training do the adults need in order to prepare to mentor? Since the format of the Koinonia Group meetings will be much like that of the Unity

Fellowship Group meetings, the main preparation will be that of becoming comfortable with small group dynamics within an interactive context. Media resources are being accumulated and a workshop is being planned.

10. Can we choose our adult partners for the Koinonia Groups? Parents and other adults are being sought as leaders and assistants for the Koinonia Groups. It is hoped that the Koinonia Group meetings will also serve as observational training time for the assistants. Within this framework the choice of adult partners will be honored.

11. Is the pilot program representative of what the Koinonia Groups will be like next year? Not completely, but it is probably the best that can be done. The students are all volunteers and most have a high degree of spiritual motivation. We can only meet during lunch hours, which is a distraction that we will not have next year. The Unity Fellowship Groups will only meet with the pilot program students for four Tuesdays, directing their discussions on topics that the students have already chosen.

12. What will be the student composition of the Koinonia Groups? One fourth of the group will be from each class and the students will remain with the same group for their high school career. An attempt will be made to place spiritually mature student leaders in each group.

13. Are other Lutheran high schools doing this? Two Lutheran high schools in the St.Louis area already

have similar programs. On-site observation of their programs will be made in order to learn from their experiences. While many Lutheran high schools were contacted, only these two were identified in the responses that were received.

The Pilot Program

The committee that monitored the development of the Koinonia ministry approved of this approach to mentoring and recommended the start of a pilot program during the lunch hours for the last half of the school year. All faculty members were assigned to small groups, called Unity Fellowship Groups (UFG's), for the 2002-2003 school year with about five or six people in each group. They were placed into groups with some diversity of departments and gender. It was intentionally planned that they would have an opportunity to get to know faculty members that they would not otherwise be closely associated with during the regular school activities. These groups were intended to be models for the student Koinonia groups that would be formed the following school year. From each group one member was assigned the responsibility of being the facilitator. At the first faculty meeting of the school year the new ministry was presented to the faculty which was generally met with approval.

The pilot program, with about forty-five students, began in the second semester. They met during their lunch hours with about fifteen students in each of the three lunch periods. They were mostly sophomores and juniors with a few freshmen. They were organized into small groups with each student taking a turn at leading. They worked with the understanding that they would be the core of the leadership for the next school year. The following topics were listed by the group as being significant for them.

Topics Suggested for the Koinonia Pilot Program

These are listed in the order of frequency of suggestion.

- Priorities and decisions
- Friendships and cliques
- Parents
- Judging others, hypocrisy, and respect
- Worship styles
- Stress
- Understanding the leading of the Holy Spirit
- War
- Grief and suffering
- Dress
- Fighting sin in our lives
- Blasphemy and improper use of the tongue
- Dating
- Living the witnessing faith
- Loving others, even our enemies
- Working together in the church
- Prayer
- Forgiveness
- Cults
- Entertainment
- How to study God's word
- Ministry in daily life
- Doubts
- Satan

Scripture references that were relevant for those topics were prepared along with questions that could be used to elicit discussion. As other resources were discovered they were also made available to the students. During the four months that they met only about half of the topics were discussed. The groups were to begin each session with a general prayer asking for the guidance of the Holy Spirit. They also were to end each session with prayers that were requested by the members of the group. Mark and I were present to monitor their progress, to ask and field questions, and occasionally to participate ourselves.

Because the Koinonia ministry was something completely new at CLHS we knew that there would have to be many adjustments to this ministry as we proceeded. Mark and I were constantly in prayer, asking for God's guidance and asking many other people to do the same.

Preparations for the First Full Year

As we continued to work on developing mentor skills in the Unity Fellowship Groups we prepared for the full implementation of of the Koinonia ministry for the next school year. Nominations for student leaders were received from faculty and other students. Students could nominate themselves. Those students who were nominated were asked to complete an application.

Nominations for student KG leaders were received before Easter. When Mark and I tabulated all the nominations we found that nearly ninety percent of the students had been nominated, some, many times. After the faculty members had the opportunity to look over the list of nomination and to submit their evaluations of the students, the directors, together with the Koinonia support committee, made the final selection of leaders for the first year. The students who were interested enough to be part of the pilot program were automatically nominated. From those who completed the application 63 students were chosen by the committee to be trained as Koinonia group leaders.

All available adult staff members were to be utilized as mentors to keep the Koinonia groups to about twelve students each. Forty-eight faculty and administrative personnel, three secretaries, two nurses, and one librarian were considered as possibilities. The chosen leaders were then given the opportunity to choose which adult mentor they would like to work with the following year. Of course, not every leader got their first choice and some leaders had to be placed with mentors they hadn't chosen. The mentors also had the opportunity to agree to mentor the student leader with whom they were placed.

Before the end of the 2002-2003 school year a meeting with all KG leaders took place in order to orientate them to the format of the KG groups and their responsibilities as KG leaders. The entire CLHS family was made aware of the process through the daily bulletin, the weekly faculty bulletin, and through a public address announcement at the beginning of the school day.

The following year the KG leaders would be scheduled into one of two zero hour classes that would meet two times per week before school. They would receive academic credit for an extra religion elective which would be in addition to their regular junior or senior religion class.

A forum to help prepare faculty and other adults to

effectively serve as counselors for the KG groups and KG group leaders was planned. The UFG's were to be continued the same as the 2002-2003 school year with the additional objective of serving as a forum to discuss and improve effectiveness as KG counselors. A leaders' handbook was prepared, resources for the leaders class were located and purchased, and a leaders retreat was planned for the week prior to the next school year.

During this time the assistant librarian mentioned a Bible that her church was using for small groups. It was the Serendipity Bible. The one they were using was directed toward adults, but she thought they also had one for youth. A couple of examination copies of the <u>Serendipity Student Bible</u> were ordered from the Serendipity website. After a closer look we thought that it would be an exceptionally valuable resource for our Koinonia ministry. Our principal, being wholly supportive of the Koinonia ministry, found the money to buy a copy for each of the student leaders to use as well as for each mentor. The Serendipity Bible gave our Koinonia leaders a resource that could be used with a minimum of effort on the part of the leaders. It contained a section on how to use the materials to prepare for small group discussion. It also provided footnotes for understanding key words and concepts with background information, 120 lesson plans on important issues for Christian living with associated activities, Bible references, and gradually deepening discussion questions. It also listed 150 Favorite Bible Stories With Questionnaires, Additional Topics for Study, a Subject Index, and a Dictionary Concordance.

A mission statement for the Koinonia ministry was prepared so that all who were involved could move forward toward the same objective. It reads as follows: The mission of the Koinonia ministry at Concordia Lutheran High School is to pursue a closer, growing relationship with Jesus Christ and each other through small group interactive Bible study and prayer, and to increase the desire to follow God's will for our lives.

With these preparations we now felt ready to implement the Koinonia ministry for the 2003-2004 school year.

The First Full Year

The full Koinonia ministry began in the 2003 - 2004 school year with a Saturday to Sunday overnight retreat at Camp Lutherhaven in Northeastern Indiana. The leaders, who were chosen the previous school year, were told, with their acceptance letter, that they were to set aside this time for the retreat. Over fifty of the sixty-one student leaders were able to participate. The theme verse for this first year was 1Timothy 4:12. "Don't let anyone look down on you because you are young, but set an example for the believers in speech, in life, in love, in faith and in purity." Mark and I directed the retreat and a school secretary volunteered to be the chaperon for the girls. The retreat center had a large meeting area with round tables which was ideal for our discussion format. A timeline description of the activities and discussion topics for the retreat was prepared. This was distributed to all of the participants the week before the retreat. The purpose of the retreat was to build spiritual relationships between all Koinonia Leaders and to focus clearly on our objectives for the coming school year.

The camp atmosphere also provided many opportunities

to build relationships between the leaders. There was much singing, planned activities to get to know more about each others lives, spontaneous games, canoeing, swimming, and hiking in the woods. The students themselves prepared a campfire meditation with a skit, singing, and a talk by one of the very enthusiastic leaders. They all went to bed tired but couldn't resist talking late into the night in their dorm rooms.

During the first faculty meeting of the school year the adult mentors were reminded of their responsibilities with a presentation by Mark and I and were given the following list of responsibilities.

<u>Responsibilities of Faculty (Adult) Partners for Koinonia Groups</u>

Pray regularly for the specific joys, concerns, and needs of each member of the group.

Maintain a solid relationship with the student leader.

Participate in the group meetings without dominating the discussions.

Report any problems, concerns, or victories to the director.

Exhort and admonish with all love and sincerity.

Share your faith with the group.

Seek ways to enhance the role of the student leader.

Be more than an adult presence in the room.

Meet at least bi-weekly with the student leader to discuss the progress of the group.

The Koinonia leaders were commissioned during one of the early chapels in the school year. The campus pastor performed the ceremony asking the leaders to come to the front, asking them to be faithful to the Koinonia ministry and then asking the student body to be supportive of them and to work with them. A similar ceremony has been conducted each year. Myself, Mark, and one or more of the experienced leaders have usually been the speakers for this chapel service.

The Spiritual Leadership Class

The Bible was the primary text that was used for the early morning class for the Koinonia leaders. New course additions to the curriculum at CLHS take many months of advance preparation. We had planned to introduce a for-credit course for all Koinonia leaders this first year but were unable to meet the deadline the previous year. This early morning class was given without credit the first year while preparations were made to make it a credit course for the following year. A description of the course "Spiritual Leadership" follows:

> The Koinonia Group leaders, the members
> of this class, are nominated by members of
> the CLHS family, submit an application,
> evaluated by the faculty, and selected by a

special committee. The class is composed of the selected junior and senior students. This course prepares the chosen Koinonia Group leaders to serve their small groups in prayer and study of the Holy Scriptures in order to address the issues that currently confront the youth of Concordia Lutheran High School. The participant leaders will receive one religion credit. This course is in addition to the required course in religion for the junior and senior years.

This course was an elective course and was not designed to replace the regular Junior and Senior courses that the religion department offers. Mark and I thought the student leaders should be rewarded with credit for all the hours they put in for this course. Later, in the second year, after much discussion with the leaders, we discovered that the majority of the leaders did not want credit for the course, basically for two reasons. One, they thought that it should be part of their service to the high school, and two, many of the leaders were honor students and even receiving an "A" in the class would have lowered their GPA because the honors courses that they were taking allowed for an "A+", and regular credit courses, such as "Spiritual Leadership", could only give an "A" as the highest grade. The credit for the course was then made optional, but attendance continued to be mandatory.

The course began with a review of the leaders handbook that was prepared with the help of the information that Rev. Ron Roma sent to us. Appropriate alterations were made for our particular situation at CLHS. Half of the leaders met on one morning and the other half met on another morning. The leaders were expected to read the entire New Testament during the school year following a plan that was given to them. They were also asked to journal their thoughts as they read. Their journals and their experiences in leading their groups provided much of the material used for class which was very discussion oriented.

Part of the class time was also devoted to preparing for the next Koinonia meeting. In addition to their leaders Bibles, which the students brought to each class meeting, the classroom contained about thirty other books of devotions, books about leading small groups, and books about relationship building activities. During the second year the students were also supplied with a copy of *Checklist for Life: The Ultimate Handbook.* It focuses on practical issues for Christian youth as they confront life. *Checklist* contains sixty-six units for reflection, meditation, and discussion. Each unit contains relevant Scripture passages, quotes from noted Christians, a personal checklist, things to do, and things to remember. There is ample material in each unit for at least one meeting. While no discussion questions are supplied, the "Will" section can easily be made into questions that stimulate good discussion.

As a part of the class the leaders were also taught how to use several types of software to help them research the Scriptures and to develop their own Bible discussion materials. A retired executive from the Indiana District of the LCMS, prepared a number of devotions with discussion questions for their use. The students were also encouraged to search and evaluate resources in various media forms and to present them to the class.

Subsequent Years

During the school year one of the leaders designed a tee shirt and most of the leaders ordered one. The design on the front carried out the concept of "The Fruit of the Spirit" which was the theme verse for this second year. The back of the shirt contained a list of the names of all of the leaders and the school year. A different shirt, designed by a leader, was prepared for each of the next two years.

The students were constantly reminded that each Koinonia meeting, regardless of the format, must include prayer and an examination of the Scriptures. Each leaders class began with specific prayer requests and ended with a general prayer which was usually spoken by one of the students. The students also had time to meet in small groups and to discuss their concerns and successes and to pray for each other.

In preparation for the second year the Juniors who had been leaders were automatically nominated to be leaders again. They were required, however, to once again submit an application. This time nominations were not actively sought from the whole high school student body. The teachers and student leaders were asked to submit nominations. A general announcement was again made to the entire student body through the morning announcements over the PA system and through the daily bulletin. Students could also nominate themselves.

Because we were trying to keep as many students together as possible for their entire time at CLHS, returning leaders were generally placed in the same group. The mentors were also given the opportunity to select a leader for the following year if they had been working with a Senior. Very few of the previous year's leaders had to be moved because of incompatibility with their mentors.

The second year of Koinonia began with a retreat at the high school for all leaders. The leaders and the directors ate together and did a few relationship activities. Our principal again greeted the leaders and assured them of the importance of the Koinonia ministry to the spiritual life of CLHS. Each leader was given a copy of the leaders handbook which was then reviewed. The previous year's leaders were given the opportunity to lead discussions about their experiences.

During this year a Koinonia council of seven of the most mature leaders was chosen. They met once each month with Mark and I at an area restaurant on a Sunday evening. The members of the council took turns leading a short devotion and speaking the prayer requests. One of the purposes of the meetings was to discuss the Koinonia ministry and to suggest new activities that might be tried. The directors also had an opportunity to have these leaders evaluate some of the ideas they had for improving the ministry.

The early morning leaders class began much like that of the first year and continued the same through the first semester. This year a mid-year retreat was held at Concordia Theological Seminary. The Koinonia Council members took much responsibility for conducting the retreat and the leading the discussions. It was at this meeting that the leaders brought up the suggestion that the grade for the leaders class should be made optional. Originally it had been thought that academic credit for the class would be a reward for their work. The directors then brought this issue to the next meeting of the Koinonia support committee. By this time the leaders had about all the training that they needed so it was decided to make the grade optional. The early morning meetings were changed to once per week with all members to be in attendance. The meetings were then held in the small meditation chapel at CLHS.

The third year of Koinonia again began with a day long retreat at the high school. The retreat activities were similar to that of the second year. The devotion was based on the theme of the year which was taken from 2Peter 3:18 - "Grow in the grace and knowledge of our Lord and Savior Jesus Christ." Prayers, Scripture meditation, relationship building activities, food, and fellowship were again the main components of the retreat.

This year we continued meeting on Wednesday mornings with the whole group as we did for the last half of the previous year. All of the new leaders were required to come to an extra morning session to receive extra training. This continued for the first quarter. During this time the leaders handbook was carefully examined and discussed. The new leaders were given training in preparing good discussion questions and they tried out these questions on each other in small groups. They were also given the opportunity to discuss issues that came up in their meetings.

On Wednesday mornings the leaders were organized into seven small groups with a Koinonia Council member as the facilitator in each group. Each leader first chose an accountability partner and then they chose the leader they would be with. The general format of these meetings was first to discuss the previous week's Koinonia meeting, then have a short devotion on a verse that was often given to them, and finally they closed in prayer using a format of their own choosing.

The fourth year theme was "Each one should use whatever gift he has received to serve others, faithfully administering God's grace in its various forms." (1Peter 4:10) Going along with this theme the Koinonia Council members took on a much larger role at the opening year retreat, which was again held at the high school. They prepared a skit which somewhat humorously depicted some of the problems that might come up in a Koinonia meeting. They also prepared five mini-sessions which were each about seventeen minutes long, which was the time allotted for each Koinonia meeting this year.

During the fourth year Mark and I traded places. He became the lead director and I became his assistant. This was in preparation for my retirement at the end of the fourth year of Koinonia and the end of my forty-four years in the classroom at Concordia. During the first three years Mark led a Koinonia group and I monitored the groups by looking in on them from the halls, being as unobtrusive as possible. In this fourth year I took a Koinonia group and Mark did the monitoring.

The fifth year of Koinonia began much like the fourth year. The school principal was Mark's assistant during this year. The Koinonia theme for this year was the same as the overall school theme: "Ezra had devoted himself to the study and observance of the Law of the LORD, and to teaching its decrees and laws in Israel." (Ezra 7:10) The retreat format was very similar to that of the fourth year. The Wednesday morning meetings for the leaders were dropped and more emphasis was placed on attending the Wednesday lunch meetings together. For the fourth and fifth years Koinonia met on Mondays instead of Thursdays. During the sixth year they moved the meetings back to Thursdays in order to once again be able to reflect on the previous day's worship in chapel.

During this fifth year I continued to meet with Mark periodically for prayer and discussions about Koinonia. I was also present on Koinonia days to substitute if I was needed and to meet with Mark. I also prepared a two day presentation to be given in the sophomore religion classes since most of the new leaders for the next year come out of the sophomore class. We praise God that He has continued to provide leaders for the fifty-nine small groups the ministry requires. During the sixth year it appears that we were even able to have two leaders for most of the groups.

The faculty and staff small groups (called Unity Fellowship Groups or UFGs) continued throughout these years with varying degrees of attention paid to it. They generally met during their lunch hours, but some have found other times to meet. Some of the groups were very faithful and found much encouragement and support for each other in their faith, in their mentoring, and in their ministry. During this fifth year I also met with most of the UFGs to evaluate how they were doing and to elicit suggestions on how these meetings could be made more effective. We are still firmly convinced that a small group ministry for students will not go well unless the mentors themselves are also in small groups of their own.

Each year Concordia High School uses one school day to go out into the local community to do service activities. They work at nursing homes, churches, shelters, hospitals, homes of the elderly or handicapped, and the headquarters of various charitable organizations. The Koinonia leaders make the contacts, plan the transportation, and prepare a time of bonding activities for a long lunch break. These days have proven to be an important factor in developing closer relationships between all the members of the group.

During more than six years, Mark and I worked very closely with each other to initiate and develop the Koinonia ministry. During all of our many meetings we always included prayers for the Koinonia ministry, Concordia High School, and for the specific concerns and joys that were part of our own lives. The following Scripture passage has meant much to us during these years as we grew together as close brothers in the Lord, working together in His kingdom.

"Two are better than one, because they have a good return for their work: If one falls down, his friend can help him up. But pity the man who falls and has no one to help him up!" (Ecclesiastes 4:9-10)

In Summary

The Koinonia ministry at CLHS is a different approach to developing Biblical understanding and applications of the Scriptures to the daily lives of our young people. They still have their regular classes in religion, chapels, and classroom devotions. With the addition of this student-led, adult mentored ministry, they now have a venue in which to have meaningful interactions within the context of prayer and Scripture. It also provides a training ground for the next generation of leaders for our church.

The Koinonia ministry helps to encourage relationships

based on a Gospel orientation toward life. The format intentionally seeks an interactive relationship between both God and each other. It is intended to be a fellowship of redeemed sinners seeking to follow God's will for their lives. Under the influence of an experienced Christian as a mentor they seek to bring their faith from the knowledge realm into the sphere of daily Christian living.

Koinonia is more than a fellowship with other people who happen to be Christians. It is a fellowship based on the belief in Christ's promise to be with us always (Matthew 28:20). It is a fellowship with the active presence of the promised Holy Spirit. Through prayer and Scripture the members of the group carry on a dialogue with their God who loves them, provides for them, and guides them for fruitful living.

The specific learning objective of the Koinonia ministry at CLHS is the application of faith to the students' everyday life. Within this environment students have the opportunity to talk about issues that are current and for which they have a sense of relevance. The mentors and directors also have the opportunity to lead them inductively into Scriptures that speak to their situation. The practice of seeking answers from God, through prayer and the examination of Scripture is a habit that is essential for all Christians throughout their earthly journey.

JESUS AND THE FIVE HOLY HABITS

To the Jews who had believed him, Jesus said, "If you hold to my teaching, you are really my disciples." (John 8:31)

Jesus replied, "Anyone who loves me will obey my teaching. My Father will love them, and we will come to them and make our home with them. Anyone who does not love me will not obey my teaching. These words you hear are not my own; they belong to the Father who sent me. (John 14:23-24)

Scripture

Therefore everyone who hears these words of mine and puts them into practice is like a wise man who built his house on the rock. (Matthew 7:24)

To the Jews who had believed him, Jesus said, "If you hold to my teaching, you are really my disciples. Then you will know the truth, and the truth will set you free." (John 8:31-32)

Prayer

But when you pray, go into your room, close the door and pray to your Father, who is unseen. Then your Father, who sees what is done in secret, will reward you.

(Matthew 6:6)

Fellowship

When he had finished washing their feet, he put on his clothes and returned to his place. "Do you understand what I have done for you?" he asked them. You call me 'Teacher' and 'Lord', and rightly so, for that is what I am. Now that I, your Lord and Teacher, have washed your feet, you also should wash one another's feet. I have set you an example that you should do as I have done for you. Very truly I tell you, no servant is greater than his master, nor is a messenger greater than the one who sent him. Now that you know these things, you will be blessed if you do them. (John 13:12-17)

A new command I give you: Love one another. As I have loved you, so you must love one another. By this everyone will know that you are my disciples, if you love one another. (John 13:34-35)

Service

You are the salt of the earth. But if the salt loses its saltiness, how can it be made salty again? It is no longer good for anything, except to be thrown out and trampled underfoot.

(Matthew 5:13)

Witness

You are the light of the world. A town built on a hill cannot be hidden. Neither do people light a lamp and put it under a bowl. Instead they put it on its stand, and it gives light to everyone in the house. In the same way, let your light shine before others, that they may see your good deeds and glorify your Father in heaven. (Matthew 5:14-16)

Printed in the United States
By Bookmasters